TWO STATES—
ONE NATION?

Other books by Günter Grass

GÜNTER GRASS

TWO STATES— ONE NATION?

Translated from the German by
KRISHNA WINSTON *with* A. S. WENSINGER

A HELEN AND KURT WOLFF BOOK
HARCOURT BRACE JOVANOVICH, PUBLISHERS
San Diego   New York   London

HBJ

Copyright © 1990 by Luchterhand Literaturverlag GmbH, Frankfurt am Main
English translation copyright © 1990 by Harcourt Brace Jovanovich, Inc.

The excerpts from these works by Günter Grass are all reprinted by permission of Harcourt
Brace Jovanovich, Inc.: *Dog Years* (Hundejahre), copyright © 1963 by Hermann Luchterhand
Verlag, GmbH, English translation copyright © 1965 by Harcourt Brace Jovanovich, Inc. and
Martin Secker and Warburg Ltd.; "Mister, Mister" in *Four Plays,* copyright © 1965 by Verlag
Klaus Wagenbach, Berlin, English translation copyright © 1967 by Harcourt Brace Jovanovich,
Inc. and Martin Secker and Warburg Ltd.; *From the Diary of a Snail* (Aus dem Tagebuch Einer
Schnecke), copyright © 1972 by Hermann Luchterhand Verlag, English translation copyright
© 1973 by Harcourt Brace Jovanovich, Inc.; *The Plebeians Rehearse the Uprising* (Die Plebejer
Proben Den Aufstand), copyright © 1966 by Hermann Luchterhand Verlag, GmbH, English
translation copyright © 1966 by Harcourt Brace Jovanovich, Inc. and Martin Secker and
Warburg Ltd.; *Selected Poems* (Gedichte von Günter Grass), translated by Michael Hamburger,
English translation copyright © 1966 by Martin Secker and Warburg Ltd.; *The Flounder* (Der
Butt), copyright © 1977 by Hermann Luchterhand Verlag, English translation copyright ©
1978 by Harcourt Brace Jovanovich, Inc.

Original titles: Deutscher Lastenausgleich. Wider das dumpfe Einheitsbegot
Reden und Gespräche—and—Schreiben nach Auschwitz

Library of Congress Cataloging-in-Publication Data
Grass Günter, 1927–
[Dautscher Lastenausgleich, English]
Two states—one nation?: against the unthinking clamor for
German reunification/by Günter Grass; translated from the German
and annotated by Krishna Winston with A. S. Wensinger.—1st ed.
p.   cm.
"A Helen and Kurt Wolff book."
Translation of: Deutscher Lastenausgleich.
ISBN 0-16-192270-6
1. German reunification question (1949–   )   2. Confederation of
states—Germany.   I. Winston, Krishna.   II. Wensinger, Arthur S.,
1926–   III. Title.
DD257.25.G6613   1990
943.087—dc20   90-42125

Designed by Camilla Filancia
Printed in the United States of America

First edition   A B C D E

CONTENTS

TWO STATES—
ONE NATION?

SHORT SPEECH BY
A ROOTLESS
COSMOPOLITAN

(1 9 9 0)

Shortly before Christmas, on my way to Lübeck from Göttingen, I was changing trains in Hamburg when a young man approached me, practically cornered me, and called me a traitor to the fatherland. He left me standing there with the phrase echoing in my ears. Then, after I had more or less calmly bought myself a newspaper, he approached me again, now with no mild threat but the statement that it was time to do away with my kind.

My initial anger I managed to shake off while still on the platform, but my thoughts kept returning to the incident as I continued on to Lübeck. "Traitor to the fatherland." The expression, paired with the term "rootless cosmopolitan,"[1] belongs to the special vocabulary of German history. Perhaps the young man was right when he spoke that way in cold rage. Isn't it true that I don't give a

---

1. A term used by the Right, in the thirties, to stigmatize German leftist intellectuals, many of whom were Jewish.

damn for a fatherland for whose sake my kind should be done away with?

The fact is, I fear a Germany simplified from two states into one. I reject this simplification, and would be much relieved if it did not come about—either because we Germans finally saw the light, or because our neighbors put their foot down.

I realize, of course, that my position will arouse protest—or, worse, hostility—and I'm thinking not only of the young man in the Hamburg railroad station. These days the *Frankfurter Allgemeine Zeitung* is making short work of those it labels leftist intellectuals. The paper's publishers aren't satisfied to see that communism is bankrupt; they want democratic socialism too to be defunct, including Dubček's dream of socialism with a human face. Our capitalists and communists have always had one thing in common: out of hand they condemn the Third Way.[2] That is why any suggestion that the German Democratic Republic and its citizens have finally achieved autonomy immediately gets shouted down with statistics on the number of people who have fled to the West. That a new identity, painfully acquired over the course of forty years of suppression, has at last asserted itself in a revolution—this is permitted to appear only in small print. The headlines meanwhile create the impression that what triumphed in Leipzig and Dresden, in Rostock and East Berlin, was not the people of the GDR but Western capitalism. And already they are cashing in.

2. A term used in the GDR for a socialist alternative to Stalinism.

Short Speech by a Rootless Cosmopolitan

No sooner does one ideology loosen its grip than another swoops down and seizes the prey. The new instrument of torture will be the market economy. If you don't toe the line, you won't get anything. Not even bananas.

No, I don't want an obscenely boastful fatherland fattened by swooping down and seizing—though I have nothing at my disposal to prevent the creation of this monster, nothing except a few ideas. Already I fear that reunification, under whatever subterfuge, is inevitable. The strong Deutschmark will see to that; the Springer press conglomerate, with its mass circulation, now in concert with Rudolf Augstein's flippant epistles in each Monday's *Spiegel,* will see to that;[3] and German amnesia will do its part.

In the end we'll number eighty million. Once more we'll be united, strong, and our voice—even if we speak softly—will be loud and clear. Eventually, because enough is never enough, we'll succeed, with our strong currency and after formal recognition of Poland's western border, in subjugating economically a large chunk of Silesia and a small chunk of Pomerania, and so once more—following the German fairy-tale pattern—we will be feared and isolated.

I am already a traitor to this fatherland. Any fatherland of mine must be more diverse, more colorful, more neigh-

3. The press conglomerate founded by the conservative Axel Springer has among its publications the daily *Die Welt* and the tabloid daily *Bild-Zeitung,* read by about five million Germans on their way to work in the morning. With TV magazines, women's magazines, family magazines, Sunday papers, and dailies, the conglomerate controls a large portion of the West German press. *Der Spiegel,* edited by its founder, Augstein, is Germany's only weekly news magazine. Its format is patterned on *Time,* but it specializes in tough investigative reporting and critical commentary.

borly—a fatherland that has grown, through suffering, wiser and more open to Europe.

It comes down to a choice between a nightmare and a dream. Why can't we help the German Democratic Republic, through the institution of a just and long overdue *equalizing of the burden,*[4] to achieve enough economic and democratic stability that its citizens will find it easier to stay home? Why do we insist on saddling the idea of a German confederation—an idea that could be acceptable to our neighbors—with vague notions borrowed from the 1848 constitutional assembly at St. Paul's in Frankfurt, or, as if we had no other choice, with the model of a super–Federal Republic? Isn't a German confederation already more than we ever dared hope for? An all-embracing unity, expanded territory, concentrated economic power—is this the goal we should pursue, or isn't all that far too much?

Since the mid-sixties, in speeches and articles I have spoken out against reunification and in favor of a confederation. Here, once more, I will answer the German Question. Briefly—not in ten points, but in five:

1. A German confederation puts an end to the postwar relationship of the two German states, that of one foreign country to another. It eliminates a vile border that also has divided Europe; at the same time it respects the concerns, even fears, of Germany's neighbors by constitutionally renouncing the goal of unifying into a single state.

---

4. *Lastenausgleich* refers to legislation passed in postwar West Germany that levied a tax on property that had survived the war, the proceeds going to help refugees and expellees from the eastern provinces get established in the West.

2. A confederation of two German states does not do violence to the postwar evolution of either state. Rather, it permits something new: an independent togetherness. At the same time, a confederation is sufficiently sovereign to fulfill both states' obligations to their respective alliances, thereby reinforcing the European security concept.

3. A confederation of two German states dovetails better with the current process of European integration than does a single powerful state, since an integrated Europe will itself be confederate in structure and must therefore transcend the traditional divisions into nation-states.

4. A confederation of two German states points the way to a new, different, and desirable self-definition that would include joint responsibility for German history. This understanding of cultural nationhood takes up where the efforts of the St. Paul's assembly failed. It implies a modern, broader concept of culture, and embraces the multiplicity of German culture without needing to assert unity in the sense of a nation-state.

5. A confederation of the two states that make up the German cultural nation would provide an example for the solution of different yet comparable conflicts throughout the world, whether in Korea, Ireland, Cyprus, or the Middle East—wherever one political entity has aggressively established borders or seeks to extend them at the expense of another. A German confederation could become a model to emulate.

A few additional comments. A unified German state existed, in varying sizes, for no more than seventy-five years:

as the German Reich under Prussian rule; as the Weimar Republic, precarious from the outset; and finally, until its unconditional surrender, as the Greater German Reich. We should be aware—as our neighbors are—of how much grief this unified state caused, of what misfortune it brought to others and to ourselves as well. The crime of genocide, summed up in the image of Auschwitz, inexcusable from whatever angle you view it, weighs on the conscience of this unified state.

Never before in their history had the Germans brought down upon themselves such terrifying shame. Until then, they were no better and no worse than other peoples. But the megalomania born of their complexes led them to reject the possibility of being a cultural nation within a federation and to insist instead on the creation of a unified state in the form of a Reich—by any and all means. This state laid the foundation for Auschwitz. It formed the power base for the latent anti-Semitism that existed in other places as well. It helped provide an appallingly firm foundation for the racial ideology of National Socialism.

There is no way to avoid this conclusion. Anyone thinking about Germany these days and looking for an answer to the German Question must include Auschwitz in his thoughts. That place of terror, that permanent wound, makes a future unified German state impossible. And if such a state is nevertheless insisted upon, it will be doomed to failure.

More than two decades ago in Tutzing the notion of "change through rapprochement" was formulated; argued over for a long time, the concept eventually proved correct.[5] By now, rapprochement has become accepted policy. In the GDR, change has occurred as a result of the revolutionary will of the people. What hasn't changed yet is the Federal Republic of Germany, whose people have been watching the events over there with a mixture of admiration and conde- scension: "We don't want to tell you what to do, but . . ."

Already they are poking their noses in. Help—real help—is given only on West German terms. Property, yes, they say, but no "people's property," please. The western ideology of capitalism, which aims to wipe out every other kind of ideological ism, announces, as if holding a gun to the East Germans' head: A market economy or else.

And who wouldn't put up his hands and surrender to the blessings of one whose lack of human decency is so plainly outweighed by his strength and success? I am afraid that we Germans will also let this second chance for self- definition slip by. To be a cultural nation in confederative pluralism apparently does not satisfy us; and "rapproche- ment through change" is asking too much—because it's too expensive. But the German Question can't be solved by working it out in marks and pfennigs.

What was it that young man in the Hamburg railroad station said? He was right. If sides must be drawn, let me be numbered among the rootless cosmopolitans.

---

5. "Change through rapprochement" was put forward by Egon Bahr in a 1963 speech in Tutzing. Bahr was press secretary to Chancellor Willy Brandt and became one of the architects of Brandt's *Ostpolitik*.

EQUALIZING
THE BURDEN

(1 9 8 9)

Twenty years ago Gustav Heinemann used the phrase "troublesome fatherlands," and he mentioned one by name: Germany.[1] The accuracy of his term is confirmed by recent developments. Once again it looks as though our national sanity is being swept away by a wave of inchoate nationalist emotion. With reactions that range from uneasiness to terror our neighbors are hearing Germans voice a recklessly whipped-up longing for unity.

The real news threatens to be pushed into the background: the way the people of the GDR are fighting day by day for their freedoms, chipping away, without violence, at the bastions of a hated system. A process unique in German history, because it is both revolutionary and successful. Other matters, of secondary importance, thrust themselves into the foreground. Some West German politicians push themselves

Speech given at the German Social Democratic Party (SPD) congress in Berlin, December 18, 1989, published the next day in the *Frankfurter Rundschau*.
1. Heinemann was president of the Federal Republic of Germany from 1969 to 1974.

8

onto center stage and into the limelight. While the government of the Federal Republic, led by the minister of finance, lifts the basket of goodies and glittering promises higher and higher, urging the revolutionaries in the East to attempt increasingly dangerous leaps, the federal chancellor keeps trying to focus the world's attention on himself and his ten-point program.

And this patchwork, presented in statesmanlike guise, received applause. A few sensible suggestions blinded people to the underlying tissue of contradictions and omissions (prompted by the chancellor's election strategy), to the fact that once more the unconditional recognition of Poland's western border was being withheld.

The following day brought a rude awakening. The hocus-pocus melted away. Reality — the justified alarm of Germany's neighbors, the result of long experience — caught up with the West German Bundestag. The "reunification" bubble burst, because no one in his right mind and cursed with memory can allow so much power to be concentrated in the center of Europe again. Certainly not the former Allies, playing victor again, nor the Poles, nor the French, nor the Dutch, nor the Danes. But neither can we Germans, for in a mere seventy-five years, under various executors, our unified state filled the history books of the world with suffering, ruins, defeat, millions of refugees, millions of dead, and a burden of crimes with which we will never come to terms. No one needs a second edition of this unified state, and — regardless of how benevolent we manage to appear now — such a prospect should never again be allowed to ignite the political will.

Let us learn instead from our fellow countrymen in the GDR, who, unlike the citizens of the Federal Republic, did not have freedom handed to them, but rather had to wrest it from an all-encompassing system — an accomplishment that makes us, rolling in wealth, look poor by comparison.

What justifies this arrogance of ours, flaunting its high-rise glass façades and export surpluses? What justifies this know-it-all attitude about democracy, when we've earned, at most, a "C+" on the first few lessons? What justifies our crowing over scandals across the border, when our own scandals, ranging from the *Neue Heimat* to Flick and Barschel and the Sinkhole of Celle, still stink to high heaven?[2] And what justifies the high-handedness of a Helmut Kohl compared to the modest wishes of the have-nots over there? Have we forgotten or are we repressing — practiced as we are in repression — the fact that the burden of the lost war weighed far more heavily on the smaller German state than on ours?

This is how the GDR's prospects looked after 1945, and the effects can still be felt today: no sooner had the Greater German system of tyranny lost its power than the Stalinist

2. *Neue Heimat* (New Homeland) was a housing program under the SPD revealed by *Der Spiegel* to have been used by certain members of the party and the trade unions to line their own pockets at the end of Helmut Schmidt's tenure as chancellor. Friedrich Karl Flick, head of the Flick Concern and thought to be the wealthiest man in Germany, was charged in 1984 with bribing economics minister Count Otto Lambsdorff in return for tax breaks worth hundreds of millions of marks. Uwe Barschel, the young and promising prime minister of Schleswig-Holstein elected in 1982, died, presumably of suicide, after a major political scandal. The Sinkhole of Celle: Celle is the seat of the Supreme Court of the province of Lower Saxony. In the fifties and sixties the court was notorious for shielding ex-Nazis and prosecuting communists and socialists.

system closed in, with new yet familiar forms of tyranny. Economically exploited by a Soviet Union that had previously been exploited and devastated by the Greater German Reich, confronted immediately with Soviet tanks during the workers' uprising in June 1953, and finally walled in, the citizens of the German Democratic Republic had to pay, and pay and pay again, on their own behalf as well as on the behalf of the citizens of the Federal Republic. They unfairly bore the brunt of the Second World War, which had been lost by all Germans.

So we owe them a good deal. What is called for is not a patronizing short-term loan or a shrewd buy-out of the "bankrupt GDR's assets," but rather a far-reaching equalization of the burden—due immediately and with no preconditions. A reduction in military spending and a special graduated tax levied on every citizen of the Federal Republic can finance the payment of this debt. I expect my party, the German Social Democratic Party, to make this just, overdue, and self-evident equalizing of the burden its own cause and to present it as a top-priority demand in the Bundestag.

Our fellow countrymen in the GDR are exhausted, they are in up to their necks, yet they continue fighting for their freedom, inch by inch. Not until they receive what they deserve from us can they speak and negotiate with us as equal partners about Germany and Germany, two states with one history and one culture, two confederated states within the European house. The prerequisite for self-determination is complete independence, and that includes economic independence.

Once we rid ourselves of the illusion of reunification, with its seductive but ultimately worthless rhetoric, it becomes clear that the contractual arrangement proposed by GDR prime minister Hans Modrow does indeed fit the actual situation as well as the more distant prospects.[3] Under such an arrangement, commissions with equal representation from each state could settle the obvious problems in the areas of transportation, energy, and postal service, and also settle the equalizing of the burden that is incumbent on the FRG and owed to the GDR. They could undertake the gradual dismantling of the defense budget as a means to guarantee peace. They could then coordinate development aid to the Third World, a joint German responsibility. They could also enrich Herder's concept of the cultural nation by infusing it with new content. And, not least of all, they could halt the destruction of the environment, which in any case respects no boundaries.

These and other efforts will, if successful, set the stage for further German-German rapprochements and thus smooth the way toward a confederation of the two states. But confederation, if really desired, will require the renunciation of a unified state in the sense usually implied by "reunification."

Unification in the form of annexing the GDR would result in irremediable losses: the citizens of the state that was swallowed up would be left with nothing of their painfully fought-for and won identity. Their history would fall

---

3. At a summit meeting with West German chancellor Kohl in Leipzig in 1989, Modrow requested aid from the FRG and voiced fears about reunification. He demanded assurances on the borders with Poland.

victim to the mindless clamor for unity. And nothing would be gained but a troubling abundance of power and the lust for more power. In spite of all our assurances, even the sincere ones, we Germans would become, once again, something to be feared. Our neighbors would draw away from us with distrust, and the feeling of being isolated would rear its head, giving rise to the dangerous self-pity that sees itself as "surrounded by enemies." A reunited Germany would be a colossus loaded with complexes, standing in its own way and in the way of European integration.

On the other hand, a confederation of the two German states and their explicit renunciation of a unified state would further the integration of Europe, which itself will be confederative in nature.

As a writer to whom the German language means the ability to transcend borders, I find, whenever I analyze political statements critically, that I come up against this dread either-or, all-or-nothing principle. Yet we do have a third possibility for answering the German Question. I expect my party to recognize this possibility and to make it a political reality.

For decades the Social Democratic Party, because it remains mindful of history, has been the architect and pacesetter of a policy for Germany that is oriented toward peace. Now that communist dogma has gone bankrupt, it becomes clear—if it was not clear before—that democratic socialism has a future all over the world. I must confess that the return of Alexander Dubček to the political arena moved me deeply, but it also confirmed me in my political thinking. The transformation underway in Eastern and Central Europe should give us social democrats new energy, which we need. Too often our power to act has been paralyzed by the voicing of doubts. The nineties demand that we manifest the will to shape the course of political events. In our history, the German social democrats have sometimes kept this will under house arrest, yet often enough they have displayed it, too—from August Bebel to Willy Brandt. Now, Hans-Jochen Vogel, it is your turn.[4]

4. Vogel was chairman of the SPD at this time.

MUCH FEELING,
LITTLE AWARENESS

A Conversation with Der Spiegel

(1 9 8 9)

DER SPIEGEL: Mr. Grass, twenty-eight years ago, on the day after the building of the Wall, you wrote an open letter to your fellow writer in the GDR, Anna Seghers. In it you expressed your shock at seeing the Vopos, the People's Policemen, and I quote: "I went to the Brandenburg Gate and found myself face to face with naked power, which nevertheless stank of pigskin." What feelings did you have on November 9, 1989?

GRASS: I thought: A German revolution has just taken place—without bloodshed, with a clear head, and apparently successfully. This never happened before, not in our entire history.

DER SPIEGEL: The revolution was wrested from the Communist government by the wave of emigration through

First published in *Der Spiegel* 47, November 20, 1989.

Hungary, by the rush on the embassies in Prague and Warsaw. Without that pressure it never would have come about.

GRASS: The pressure was twofold. There was pressure from the emigration and pressure from the protest rallies. Those were crowds the likes of which had never been seen in the streets of the GDR. On June 16 and 17 of 1953 there were only 350,000 people in the streets. That wasn't a popular uprising but a workers' uprising. The event was falsified in both parts of Germany—over there they said it was a counterrevolution and here it was made into a popular uprising by Adenauer's linguistic fiat.

DER SPIEGEL: You don't seem altogether happy about this revolution.

GRASS: The order in which the changes took place was wrong. The internal process of democratization should have been pushed further, before the opening of the borders was announced. The local elections should have been repeated. That would have led to a restructuring of the GDR at a higher level and given the opposition groups more room to maneuver. They could have gained the practical experience in politics that many lack.

DER SPIEGEL: So you are ambivalent?

GRASS: Ambivalent in the sense that I am not sure that in its present condition this smaller German state will survive the open border. And I am afraid, too, that in the Federal

Republic the clamor for reunification will erupt again, in the absence of workable alternative models.

DER SPIEGEL: But according to the conservative interpretation, the Basic Law [1] insists on reunification.

GRASS: There's nothing about reunification in the Basic Law. The preamble speaks of the unity of the Germans, and I'm all in favor of that.

DER SPIEGEL: You're saying, then, that anyone who talks about the reunification statute in the constitution simply does not know the constitution?

GRASS: . . . does not know the constitution or, if he knows it, is speaking against his own better judgment.

DER SPIEGEL: Which would you assume in the case of Helmut Kohl?

GRASS: I think the federal chancellor doesn't know the constitution. A quick reading of it would show him that the concept of unity allows many things, makes many things possible. More than these either-or demands, which have already wreaked such havoc in Germany. One side sticks lazily to the status quo and says, "For reasons of security in Central Europe the two-state arrangement must be preserved." And the other side calls for reunification, with no

1. *Das Grundgesetz,* the constitution of West Germany.

regard for what the moment requires. But in between lies
the possibility of achieving an accord between the two German states. Such an accord would satisfy the German need
for self-definition, and our neighbors could also accept it.
Thus, no concentration of power in the sense of reunification, and no further uncertainty from a two-state arrangement, where one foreign country confronts another. Rather,
a confederation of the two states, requiring a new definition.
It doesn't help to look back to the German Reich, whether
with the borders of 1945 or 1937; all that is gone. We have
to redefine ourselves.

DER SPIEGEL: But since the Wars of Liberation,[2] a German
accord has always been understood to imply a nation, a
common state.

GRASS: Not at all. In 1848, at the constitutional assembly at
St. Paul's in Frankfurt, many different models were discussed. I prefer to invoke Herder's concept of the cultural
nation.

DER SPIEGEL: But the confederation idea doesn't have an
immaculate past, either.

GRASS: How so?

DER SPIEGEL: Ulbricht's confederation plans of the fifties
and sixties scared the daylights out of the young Federal
Republic.

2. The German term for the Napoleonic Wars.

GRASS: We'd be giving Ulbricht too much credit if in retrospect we conceded that he came up with a workable plan. Confederation exists in many democratic states. The two German states also seem suited for confederation for other reasons. In spite of certain difficulties, the federal principle in the Federal Republic has yielded only positive results, and I wish that in the GDR, too, the old provinces would resurface in the coming years.

DER SPIEGEL: Wouldn't your charge of laziness have to apply to your SPD friend Egon Bahr, who did say, after all, "For God's sake, let's not tamper with these two states"?

GRASS: Laziness is the last thing I would charge Egon Bahr with; he used to be one of our most active minds. That's where I begin to be critical. I think Bahr, too, was surprised by this sudden development—which says nothing against him. Following his "policy of small steps," he always concentrated on safeguarding each small success. That's why he won't tamper with the existing two-state arrangement. But reunification, even with the best intentions, will push us into isolation. And when Germany feels isolated, we know what the reaction is: panic.

DER SPIEGEL: But if the GDR were linked to us in a confederation, wouldn't it become a satellite of the EEC?

GRASS: I refuse to see everything in black-and-white terms. On the one side, the completely ruined socialist-communist economy; on the other, the solid rock of capitalism. Even capitalism takes on different forms in different countries. You can adapt capitalism to the GDR in a way that won't result in total deformation and rejection of its culture, and that won't give rise to new social unrest, perhaps with a shift to the right, such as we've had here as a result of misguided capitalist policies.

DER SPIEGEL: What can the GDR contribute to a confederation of the two German states?

GRASS: Something that may have been noticed by anyone who has spent time in the GDR, something we lack: a slower pace of life, and therefore more time to talk with people. A society of private niches—I think Günter Gaus coined the phrase—has come into being; something reminiscent of the Biedermeier period, the way it was in Metternich's day.[3] Although it may disappear with the opening to the West and to democracy.

DER SPIEGEL: You don't seriously think that this anachronistic Biedermeier ambiance can hold its own against the concentrated economic power of the West?

GRASS: In the process of focusing on the German-German question, we lose sight of the real problems of the present.

3. A former foreign editor of *Der Spiegel* and from 1974 to 1981 the representative of the FRG in East Berlin, Gaus was a close associate of Willy Brandt's and a proponent of European détente. Biedermeier is a term derived from a cartoon figure, Papa Biedermeier, who embodied the style of living adopted by the German middle class after Metternich imposed his "system" of absolutist rule on Germany and Austria in the wake of the Napoleonic Wars. The middle class withdrew into domestic life, concentrating on friends and family.

But in a matter of weeks and months they'll remind us of their presence. For instance, the rapidly spreading destruction of the environment. The hole in the ozone layer won't be made any smaller by a German rapprochement.

DER SPIEGEL: To return to your personal feelings: if you had been in the Bundestag the week before last, would you have joined in the singing of the national anthem?

GRASS: Probably yes. But with very different thoughts from those who began the singing. I would guess they had reunification in mind. Our anthem is already being inflated, and that I must warn against, particularly when you consider the words of the song, which still mean something.

DER SPIEGEL: You're thinking of the third stanza?

GRASS: Yes. Unity and Justice and Freedom, those are principles that apply to both states. The GDR can give us something, a higher purpose. Are things all that wonderful here? Does what our constitution says match what we have in reality? Can a poor man, or one who isn't well-off, get his legal point across and find justice in our courts? Can a man obtain justice in the Federal Republic without high-priced lawyers? Doesn't inequity exist to a scandalous degree in this rich land? Don't we have, therefore, every reason to take the new, nonviolent, revolutionary idealism emanating from the GDR and make it our own?

DER SPIEGEL: Learning from the GDR?

GRASS: On the fourth of November on Alexanderplatz I saw all kinds of very appropriate banners, most of them referring to the situation in the GDR. But among them was one that didn't apply just to the GDR: "Cut down the big shots, save the trees." We have big shots here, too. And trees, too, that need to be saved. An all-German slogan, if you will. I've seldom seen the problem of our dual existential situation so concisely put.

DER SPIEGEL: Are you afraid that the big shots in the Federal Republic will become more ensconced and smug the worse things are in the GDR?

GRASS: I'll give you one example: Mr. Lambsdorff, a man with something of a record, chairman of a democratic party, and not sicklied o'er with self-doubt of any kind. He wants to see big reforms in the GDR before he loosens the purse strings. This man, with his past and his self-satisfied attitude, was a big shot who had to be cut down so the trees could be saved.

DER SPIEGEL: So far the GDR is the only German state where socialism has been tried. The experiment now seems to be coming to an end.

GRASS: But look at the conditions under which the experiment took place. This little state has had to bear most of the burden of the lost war. All those years, up to today. That alone obliges us to provide assistance as unselfishly as possible. The GDR had to rebuild under far more difficult conditions than we did, under a centralized bureaucracy incapable of running an economy, under the burden of Stalinism, and without the Marshall Plan, and with far more reparations to pay. The experiment failed for those reasons, and for others.

But attempts are being made within the GDR opposition—not only in the newly founded Social Democratic Party, but also in the New Forum and the group Democracy Now—to develop democratic socialism. After all, there isn't a shred of proof that the collapse of this economic system, which improperly called itself socialism, has also put an end to the experiment of democratic socialism in Germany. Such a thesis has no basis in fact and is clearly directed against the social democrats.

DER SPIEGEL: Does Günter Grass the social democrat have any explanation for the fact that the social democrats, of all people, are so speechless at this turn of events?

GRASS: I think the social democrats allowed their successful "policy of small steps" to blind them to developments that are really more leaps than steps. But the social democrats are no longer speechless. It was annoying that for a while they were. Yes, the announcement that the Social Democratic Party was being reestablished in the GDR caused confusion at first, and was met with a lack of understanding—"Must it be now?" or "Is this the right moment?" The only ones who spoke were those with misgivings.

DER SPIEGEL: But how is it that a party like the SPD, which after all has so many experts on German affairs, bet so heavily on the wrong horse—that is, on the SED, the communist party of the GDR?

GRASS: I don't see it that way. It was no mistake to maintain contacts with the SED. I believe it is wrong to rely exclusively on SED contacts instead of holding them in reserve and at the same time offering sympathy and solidarity where appropriate to support what is emerging and happening in the country.

DER SPIEGEL: Apparently in shock at the end of the Honecker era, Norbert Gansel coined the slogan "change through maintaining distance."[4]

GRASS: I don't think he would put it that way today. But his critique was justified.

DER SPIEGEL: So the fact remains: the SPD doesn't have a clear policy on Germany.

GRASS: The party established ties with GDR officials at the right time, and then worked out something that was useful not only for the SPD-SED relationship but also for the entire population. Because of this jointly formulated document it was easier for the opposition to define itself and to get where it is today.

4. Norbert Gansel, a lawyer, since 1986 the head of the SPD party council.

DER SPIEGEL: Helmut Kohl said the constitution of the Federal Republic didn't allow him to speak for all Germany, and thus didn't allow him to recognize the western border of Poland.

GRASS: In saying that, he denies Chancellor Willy Brandt's right to have concluded the Warsaw treaties, treaties which Kohl also invokes. He's buttering up the Christian Democratic Union, specifically its right wing. It's fear of the Republicans [5] that's preventing Kohl from uttering this long overdue, liberating, and essential guarantee. And that's the real scandal, because he won't get a second chance.

Something also should be said about the embarrassing nature of the chancellor's trip to Poland. About the narrow-mindedness of the man, his refusal to learn, his know-it-all attitude—this man is simply unbearable as federal chancellor. I don't know who advised him to visit the Annaberg; the only positive thing is that the younger generation got a belated history lesson by asking what actually happened there. How Poles were shot by German Free Corpsmen, who were also active elsewhere. I don't know what other tasteless and insensitive actions will occur to Mr. Kohl in the future. In this respect his behavior in office has been consistent.

DER SPIEGEL: Why is it that intellectuals in the Federal Republic have so little to say about the German Question?

5. *Die Republikaner,* a radical right-wing group that came to prominence in the FRG in the late eighties.

GRASS: There's no simple answer. Many factors may be involved. The culture business in the Federal Republic diverts a lot of energy; it's a well-funded business that seduces people into self-absorption. Then there are certain trends that have been particularly well received by the critics, for instance, a self-absorbed literature, for which you can certainly make an argument. It isn't likely writers will stop focusing on themselves, and come to see themselves instead in the context of a society or historical movement, to see themselves as contemporaries. That's how I see myself, as a contemporary. Which is what has made me speak out again and again, whether I wanted to or not.

Just recently I recalled a talk I was invited to give before the Bonn Press Club in the late sixties or early seventies, and which aroused much opposition at the time. It was called "The Communicating Plural." I tried to formulate, in words different from the ones I use today, a notion of how the GDR and the FRG could coexist side by side. In *Headbirths* I not only dealt with the Third World but kept returning to what was on my own doorstep; in that book my idea of the cultural nation was sketched for the first time.

DER SPIEGEL: Besides you, only your colleague Martin Walser is kept awake at night by the topic of Germany. He broods: "When I think of Königsberg, I find myself in a vortex of history that whirls me around and swallows me up."[6]

6. Königsberg, the birthplace of Kant, formerly in East Prussia, since 1946 has been Kaliningrad, a Russian city.

GRASS: That's too much feeling and too little awareness.

DER SPIEGEL: He thinks it's a feeling for history.

GRASS: Well, of course, it's a pain that I, too, will carry around with me all my life. Having an awareness of history or developing it doesn't mean one has no feelings. When I go to Gdańsk and look for traces of Danzig, I'm never free of feelings. Which often leads to arguments, because just as I speak out against German chauvinism, I speak out against Polish chauvinism.

But I'm also proud that my hometown has started something. When I was in Gdańsk again in 1981, and my graphic works were on exhibit, the mayor made a little speech in German and said something like, "A son of our city has achieved international renown. We are proud of him." I have these feelings, too, but it doesn't make me maudlin. And this is where I'd criticize Walser. But it's a good thing that he expresses himself—even if I'm of a different opinion—and gets involved in the discussion and stirs up debate. I prefer that to the stuffy silence of those who dodge the subject altogether.

DER SPIEGEL: But this earned him an invitation from the Christian Democratic Union to attend its closed meeting in Wildbad Kreuth, where he played *Schafskopf* with Theo Waigel, who insists on the 1937 borders.[7]

7. *Schafskopf,* a German card game. The word also means a fool. Theodor Waigel, West German minister of finance since 1989, became leader of the conservative CSU (Christian Social Union), the Bavarian branch of the CDU (Christian Democratic Union). He advocated Germany's return to the borders of 1937.

GRASS: That's something Walser has to settle with himself. What to me seems more problematical is that a writer with a memory—a prerequisite for a writer—who in 1967, at the last meeting of Group 47, demanded a boycott of the Springer newspapers and worked hard for it, should be one of the first to break the boycott.[8] That hurt me.

Of course, Walser has a right to change his mind. When I met him, he was a clever conservative from Lake Constance with a certain cautious leaning toward the Social Democratic Party. During the student protests he edged toward the German Communist Party, then pulled back again, and now he's chatting with Waigel. There are a few too many unexplained twists there, and I don't like them. Much of Walser's marvelously articulate spirit of contradiction is now left in the dust; he's gone flat, maudlin, as happens when intellectuals turn sentimental.

DER SPIEGEL: The lack of interest in a national policy doesn't bode well for your cultural nation.

GRASS: Well, it's different in the GDR. I'm thinking of Christoph Hein, for instance. And there are authors like Erich Loest, who in the meantime have come to live in the Federal Republic. I could name a good number of writers who, on the basis of their biography, their experiences either

8. Group 47 was a loose association of authors, critics, and publishers brought together by Hans Werner Richter for yearly meetings, providing a forum for the reading and discussion of new work. It functioned from 1947 to 1967 and exerted considerable influence on German postwar literature.

in one or the other or both states, are certainly in a position to lend content to the idea of a cultural nation.

DER SPIEGEL: Peter Schneider wonders about the post-Wall future: "Can we exist without an enemy?"

GRASS: I think that at the moment the West is having trouble living without the image of an enemy. Industry in the West is reluctant to say good-bye to the whole armaments program. For decades people felt threatened by the armaments potential of the Soviet Union and the satellite countries—as they used to be called, and not without reason. They justified rearmament that way, and it escalated. But now that disarmament has begun over there, a response on our side is lacking. We still insist on the necessity of NATO in its present form. No transformation is taking place. Here Gorbachev's saying fits: "He who arrives late is punished by life."

DER SPIEGEL: Mr. Grass, thank you for talking with us.

SHAME AND DISGRACE

On the Fiftieth Anniversary of the Outbreak of War

(1 9 8 9)

One who rummages through the garbage heap of the past comes upon banalities. On September 1, 1939 I was an eleven-year-old hunting for bomb fragments in the Danzig suburb of Neufahrwasser, where the harbor was located. And when I couldn't find any, I traded something—I no longer remember what—for one of those jagged pieces of metal from the bombs dropped by German dive bombers over the Westerplatte, the Polish military enclave within the territory of the Free State of Danzig.

That was how the war began for me at home. I remember late summer days warm enough for swimming, and the weather held, even though the Baltic beaches remained off-limits because of the fighting that continued on the Hela peninsula. The war arrived suddenly, literally out of the clear blue sky, and it was over soon, later to be referred to as the "Polish Campaign." Oh, yes, an uncle of mine, who had participated in the defense of the Polish Post Office, was

Speech, first published in *Süddeutsche Zeitung* (Munich), September 2, 1989.

shot after a court-martial; but we didn't talk about that in the family.

This short war—like other campaigns later on that were not so short—entered my experience in a strikingly one-sided way with the help of the German newsreels. After endless columns of prisoners and shots of horse cadavers among bombed artillery emplacements, the newsreels supplied my uncomprehending mind with cuts from a victory parade never shown again. Units of the Wehrmacht and of the Red Army marched one after the other past a German and a Soviet Russian general; both generals saluted.

Poland was doubly beaten: a weak state, with inadequate leadership and an army infatuated with tradition but woefully ill-equipped, she collapsed under the blows of two modern military powers, the Wehrmacht striking first in a surprise attack and the Red Army mopping up. After that, the liquidation of the Polish elite and eventually of the Polish people developed, as planned, into a matter of routine. Between 1939 and 1946 the population shrank from thirty-five million to twenty-four million. Estimates place the number of Poles and Polish Jews who died in the war, were murdered, or starved to death, at close to seven million. Yet the attempt to murder a people who had seemed conquered and beaten to begin with did not prevent the Polish resistance from organizing right after September 1939. Soon it spread throughout the country. Even after the Warsaw Uprising collapsed, the resistance continued.

Today, after fifty years, we remember the suffering of the Poles and the disgrace of the Germans, and find that there still remains, no matter how harshly we were punished, more than enough guilt, and time has not sweetened this sediment, a sediment that cannot be washed away with fine words. Even if someday a major new effort is made to right this wrong, the shame will remain.

Shame and sorrow. Because the crime brought into the world by us Germans resulted in further suffering, further injustice, the loss of homelands. Millions of East and West Prussians, Pomeranians, and Silesians had to leave their birthplaces. This burden cannot be equalized. The war cost those Germans more than it did other Germans. This imbalance made many of the older generation bitter; some are bitter to this day.

In 1945 I, too, lost an irreplaceable part of my origin: my hometown, Danzig. I, too, took the loss hard. Time and again I had to remind myself of the reasons for it: German arrogance and disdain for human beings; German blind obedience; that German hubris which in defiance of all legality proclaimed an all-or-nothing as its will, and in the end, when everything lay buried in suffering, refused to acknowledge the nothing.

And refuses to this day. Hence my speech on shame and disgrace. For the shame is added to when West German politicians have the gall to conjure up, before a predisposed audience, the German boundaries of 1937. They seek to appease the voters on the far right. Thus Poland's western border becomes the subject of loose talk. As if Poland were not feeling shaky enough at the moment. So we take advantage of Poland's weakness. So Poland faces humiliation again at the hands of the Germans. So a German cabinet minister and party chairman is allowed to slough off shame and take disgrace in stride.[1]

Sunday speeches of this sort, calculatingly delivered to refugee associations, have a history of their own: during the fifties and sixties they formed part of a political ritual which irresponsibly and stubbornly refused to recognize the origins or accept the consequences of a war begun and lost by the Germans. "Peaceful reacquisition" and "right to a homeland" were the slogans then, repeated so often that they became empty flourishes. Millions of Poles had to leave Vilna and Lemberg after the loss of Poland's eastern provinces to the Soviet Union; they were resettled in Danzig and Breslau,[2] where they could talk about their "right to a homeland" all they liked.

Reminders of the agreements reached by the victorious Allies at Yalta and Potsdam did no good. Incorrigibly, defiantly the banners continued to declare "Silesia will stay German!" As if that province, the object of bloody battles between Prussia and Austria over the centuries, hadn't constantly changed rulers; as if Danzig, before it became Prussia's in the third partition of Poland, hadn't grown rich under three hundred years of Polish rule and kept its Hanseatic character. That all happened before Europe organized itself into nation-states, thereby providing the pretext for new wars born of the nationalism that sprang up everywhere. The bacillus of nationalism remains virulent in France, Ger-

1. A reference to Theodor Waigel. See page 27.
2. Vilna, Lemberg, and Breslau are now Vilnius, Lvov, and Wrocław.

many, and equally in Poland. Polish nationalists, whose
Polishness has degenerated into a pious arcanum, still talk
themselves into believing that the former eastern German
provinces are ancient Polish lands that they have won back.
Apparently this type of tunnel vision, which makes a virtue
of ignoring the facts of history, persists in Poland as in Germany.

Still, in spite of bitter opposition, this unreal debate was
laid to rest in December 1970, or so one was allowed to
hope: the signing of the German-Polish treaty in Warsaw
recognized Poland's western border. And because Willy
Brandt, chancellor at the time, was well aware of the his-
toric significance of this long overdue acknowledgment of
the facts, he had in his entourage, among others, two writers. Siegfried Lenz and I were there when a document valid
under international law sealed the loss of our homeland.[3]
We had long since accepted this loss; we had learned to live
with it. Many of our books dealt with it and its causes. And
yet, when we boarded the plane to Warsaw, it was not with
glad anticipation but with feet of lead. But then Willy Brandt
went down on his knees on the spot where the Jewish ghetto
had been under German rule, and it became clear that the
murder of six million Jews, planned and carried out by Germans — this crime and the extermination camps of Ghelno,
Treblinka, Auschwitz, Birkenau, Sobibor, Belżec, and Mai-
danek — could not be rectified, and our loss of a homeland
seemed insignificant.

3. Lenz was born in the East Prussian region known as Masuria, one of the territories assigned to Poland in 1945.

A few days after the signing of the German-Polish treaty came the first strike by the workers in the Polish Baltic shipyards. The militia opened fire on the workers. So the beginnings of the movement that would come to be called Solidarity a decade later go back to December 1970.

Since then Poland has had no peace. Martial law struck down the hopes of the people. Governments came and went; only the shortages were constant. Even today, shortages are accompanying the defeat of the old system and the desperate efforts of a new government, a government that was at least somewhat democratically elected.

Poland needs help, our help, for we still owe a debt to Poland. But not the sort of help that dictates conditions, that forces Polish weakness to taste German strength, that makes shameful, boastful speeches like the one given recently by the Bavarian politician Theo Waigel. September 1 should provide him with ample reason to eat his words, words that can bring only misery in their wake. Whoever calls Poland's western border into question is inciting to breach of treaty. Whoever speaks that way, whoever still speaks that way today, is acting shamefully and dragging us into disgrace.

THINKING ABOUT GERMANY

From a Conversation with Stefan Heym
in Brussels

(1 9 8 4)

GRASS: The Germans have always had trouble defining themselves as a nation. Before Bismarck got his turn and unified the country politically, creating in the process the concept of a German nation, exhaustive debates on the subject took place at St. Paul's in Frankfurt. If you look them up, you will find interesting notions, some of them formulated by German writers, Uhland for instance, which give precedence to the concept of the cultural nation as against the political nation. Certainly times have changed, and with them the definition of culture. But if we recognize that we in Germany have twice failed with our *political* idea of a nation, to our grief and that of our neighbors, it might make sense to revert to the other idea, which was never really tried.

The discussion took place November 21, 1984 (on the occasion of the twenty-fifth anniversary of the founding of the Goethe Institute) and was published unabridged in Berlin/Brussels 1984, © Günter Grass and Stefan Heym. Heym, novelist and essayist, emigrated to the United States in 1933, served in the army, and returned to the GDR in 1952.

Especially since it's become clear that one can divide everything geographically, politically, economically, yet culture, that most delicate entity, resists division most stubbornly. Take literature, for example. It can be demonstrated, to my own surprise, that the GDR hasn't succeeded in creating its own national literature. Despite the indifference in the West and the years of cultural isolationism, it hasn't been possible to stifle the interest in what is going on across the border. For a decade or more there's been a clear dialogue between one book and another, without any collusion, without specific publishing programs, let alone a joint cultural policy. The authors simply fell into conversation with each other, behind the backs of the prevailing policies.

Therefore the fact that the two of us are sitting here today is really no surprise. Government officials in comparable positions in one state or the other would have more trouble getting along, even on questions of language. We at least know that a German literature existed long before the Federal Republic and the GDR. Basically a truism, but one that many politicians, who consider their respective states the be-all and end-all, refuse to recognize. So I believe that culture, augmented by our common history, can provide a sufficiently solid foundation for us to redefine the concept of nation, down to the practical details.

People on this side probably aren't aware that for years there's been a dispute between the two German states over the so-called Prussian Cultural Holdings. What speaks against joint administration of these Prussian Cultural Holdings? Point by point, something shared, something all-German, could evolve, without a concentration of economic or even military power in the center of Europe.

And if, as Stefan Heym has thought and stated, the two states were successful in living up to their political responsibility in the center of Europe and toward neighboring states, that for me would be sufficient as the basis for a new concept of nationhood. By common political responsibility I mean this: after the experience of two world wars started by Germany, both states have an obligation to prevent future wars, to contribute more than other countries to the reduction of tensions, the tensions first of all in their own house, between Germans. And I could imagine a dialogue developing between the two states, maybe first in the area of culture, which would be an easing of tension, so that our neighbors would stop fearing, as they do now, a new concentration of power in the center of Europe. . . .

HEYM: Well, Günter Grass, I don't believe the German Question can be unraveled by way of culture. The reason I don't believe it is that culture in the GDR is viewed as part of the ideological superstructure and of ideology, which, as you know, is a monopoly of those in power. So obstacles will crop up if you come along and want to create a certain unity or uniformity on the basis of culture. Of course one should work toward it, of course one should have joint cultural events, the joint publication of books. I'm happy to hear that two books of yours will finally be appearing in my country, and I'm happy that our leaders have recognized that this won't topple the GDR. And if someday they recognize that Heym's books won't topple the GDR either, maybe they'll publish them too. . . .

You have articulated something very important, that is, the question of war and peace and what that has to do with the two German states. One thing is sure, and here I have to agree with the Frenchman who said he loved Germany so much that he was glad there were two of them . . .

It's like this: neither of the two German states by itself is in a position to start a war now. But both German states together can work toward keeping the peace. And here I'd like to say something in praise of our GDR and its leaders — and that's rare for me. You see, Honecker announced that he doesn't like having missiles in the GDR one bit. And he said that he's prepared to bring the territory of the GDR into a nuclear-free zone. I haven't heard anything of the sort from Helmut Kohl yet. And if that could come about, it would be a big step forward for us. It would be a start at defusing the distrust — the entirely justified distrust — of the Germans and certainly of the Germans united. After all, what sort of people are these, really? I brought something along —
· the only thing I plan to read aloud — that Thomas Mann wrote about the Germans:

> The German concept of freedom was always directed outward. This concept of freedom meant the right to be German, only German, and nothing else, nothing beyond that. It was a protest-ridden concept, self-centered defensiveness against anything that might circumscribe and limit racial egotism, tame it

and put it at the service of the community, of man-
kind. A stubborn individualism directed outward, it
tolerated internally a distressing lack of freedom,
immaturity, unthinking subservience.

I'd like you to remember these last three things, because
they crop up all too often—even today, in the GDR as in
the Federal Republic. And these human beings, we must try
to change them. They have to become free, learn to think
critically, and when that happens, a second big chunk of the
distrust of the Germans will be removed, those Germans
whom people always picture standing at attention.

I'd also like to describe something I saw in Göttingen. I
was looking at the display of a bookstore at the station,
where they had a series of very handsome picture books,
German Landscapes, and all those German landscapes weren't
German anymore. They'd been lost by Hitler. One of the
volumes had the title *Breslau, a German City.* As long as you
still run into things like that, you can't complain when people don't trust the Germans. . . .

GRASS: I think only one who has lost his native city or his
homeland through the fault of the Germans can speak specifically on this point. The loss remains a loss, but it must
be accepted. It's one of the reasons I chose to become active
in politics, in addition to my writing and sculpting and graphic
art—to support the Social Democratic Party when the party
began to work in that particular direction. And I went to
Warsaw along with Siegfried Lenz when the German-Polish

treaty was signed; Lenz was from East Prussia, I from Danzig. We took all kinds of abuse for it, but that was to be expected.

But today we hear politicians making noises like: "No one said this border has to be recognized for all time." And when the present chancellor doesn't whistle them back, something has to be said. Again we hear those phrases from the fifties and sixties about "peaceful reunification within the borders of 1937," borders that included East Prussia, Silesia, and Pomerania. With statements like these, no wonder the Poles are feeling apprehensive again.

True, we've had a number of political leaders who realized that we can make progress in German-German affairs only if we did what decency demands with regard to the Poles. It was Germans and the Soviet Union, the Third Reich under Hitler and the Soviet Union, that entered into a pact at the expense of Poland. Poland lost her eastern provinces and was generally shifted westward, as a result of which the Germans lost *their* eastern provinces. These are the geographical facts, and it is true that they had terrible consequences, including an expulsion of Germans that was cruel, with unnecessary atrocities that are partly understandable but nonetheless atrocities. It is an incontrovertible fact that German actions made Poland lose her eastern provinces, which in turn encouraged chauvinistic movements (the counterpart to German chauvinism) that clamored for a Polish border as far west as the Elbe; that's how bad it was. We created these facts, we must acknowledge them, and we did acknowledge them through a treaty.

But I would like to say add a few words in response to your justified doubt that a nation can be defined in terms of culture.

HEYM: Defined it certainly can be, but does that definition carry any political weight?

GRASS: Well, both German states established in 1945 have been crassly materialistic. So culture plays a validating or an ornamental role, or at least is supposed to play such a role. Its explosive force hasn't been recognized. Yet some entirely different development may make us look to culture once more. By the way, this doesn't apply only to the two German states. With rising unemployment—the result of economic and technological changes—human existence can no longer define itself exclusively through work. Other channels will be needed. And it may turn out that culture, understood in some new way, can offer such a channel, thus playing a role that goes far beyond those validating or ornamental functions attributed to it in Germany.

And when I said there was a rapprochement, a dialogue between the two German literatures, I didn't mean that a nation-culture concept should result in uniformity. It's my belief that German culture has always derived its strength from its diversity. Just as federalism is a political tradition in Germany that shouldn't be abandoned. Yes, it makes certain negotiations difficult, but cultural federalism in the Federal Republic has its advantages. And if there were such a thing in the GDR, it would be to the advantage of the GDR. There matters have been simplified Prussian-style, surely not to the benefit of culture. If we could get a joint cultural effort going now, one that draws on the diversity within both countries but also on the differences between the two regions, that would be a great gain for culture.

There are also differences between northern and southern German literature, differences in origin and in structure. And there are political differences to this day — for instance, the boundary formed by the Main River — that in some cases go deeper than the division between the GDR and the Federal Republic. So we have various political strands, each with its own ramifications, and I think this kind of open discussion of culture would yield a definition of nationhood that would allow for diversity without necessarily leading to unification. . . .

There's something else, too, and that concerns not only me; I could say this for Siegfried Lenz and Horst Bienek and many other authors who lost their geographical home. With the help of literature they have accomplished something that politicians seldom accomplish: the rescue of provinces and cities that are lost for good — through the re-creation of places and people in periods of convulsive change, of failure and of ruin. In this way writers salvage something that lives on and continues to develop, which to my mind has greater value than the politicians' attempts to conjure up with rhetoric what no longer exists, as they invariably do at meetings of refugee associations.

I experienced that in the fifties with my grandparents, who never really arrived in Lüneburg, where they lived, because they were still sitting on their suitcases. Konrad Adenauer promised them time after time: "Vote for me, and you'll return to your old home." So these people didn't even try to settle in the West. They kept thinking—with the Korean War at their backs and the Cold War in front of them—that soon they would be going home.

You know, I always thought my Kashubian aunt was right. When urged to go to the West, she shook her head and said, "In the West it's better, but in the East it's nicer."

HEYM: To get back to the subject of culture. I don't think we can solve this thing through culture alone. My dear colleague, you mention those forces in the Federal Republic that keep veering to the East. This happens, of course, because you have a social order that not only tolerates it but even encourages it.

You spoke of 1945, of coming to terms with the past. For me it was rather different: I lost my home in 1933, then in 1945 came back in an entirely different role, as a conqueror, and saw the whole thing from a different angle, and also the danger.

The question is: Where did this split come from? How did it come about? You and I were discussing it earlier today, and you said it went back to 1945. I'd say it goes a little farther back. In 1944 I was an American officer interrogating captured German officers. And a staff major said to me, "You Americans are crazy—why are you smashing our whole army? You're going to need us, and very soon, against the Russians." So here was a political idea already full-blown that later found expression, in a somewhat different form, in the division of Germany.

So that's how it came about, unfortunately. And today we have to confront the problem. The question is: How? How can these two social orders — let me use this term rather than states — forge a real link between the two German peoples?

It's perfectly clear: you wouldn't want to impose on the entire German people capitalism as it really exists in the Federal Republic — you know why I say "really exists" — with its unemployment, its drugs, its Barzels.[1] But neither would you want to impose socialism as it really exists, with its Wall and its frustrations and so on and so on. We'll have to find something that comes out of the two, we'll have to make use of elements from both: the good things about socialism — and there are all sorts of good things about it — and the things worth preserving in the West, too. They were always portrayed as capitalist by our side, but they're also simply human, no? Individual initiative, freedom to travel, etc. All that has to be kept.

It would be presumptuous of me to give a prescription. I've only just begun to think about how such a Germany should look. And I know that many other people are thinking along the same lines. In the fall of 1983 there was a series of speeches in Munich that dealt with this subject.[2] It's remarkable that all this is coming to a head now. Certainly it has something to do with what we said earlier, that

---

1. Rainer Barzel was one of the strongest opponents of Willy Brandt's coalition government (1969–1974).
2. The period of intense debate and protest that preceded the stationing of Pershing missiles with nuclear warheads in the Federal Republic.

both German populations feel threatened and are saying, "We don't want to be reunified in death."

A last question in this connection. If I say, "What kind of Germany?" should it be a Germany, for example, that has no forests left? A Germany that's completely barren? A Germany that's not worth living in anymore? The forests are dying because of socialism, of course—I was in the Erz Mountains, a sight I wouldn't want anyone to have to see. I drove over a bridge near Bernburg, and the whole river looked like shaving cream. But shaving cream is refined in comparison to the stuff floating around in that water. So economic activity in socialism creates just as much pollution and environmental destruction—which it shouldn't, that's not why we have socialism—as economic activity in capitalism, and we have to put an end to this if we want a healthy Germany, a reunified Germany that we can leave with pride to our children and their children. But I'm preaching again, it's disgusting . . .

GRASS: I'd really like to avoid the word reunification, because it implies a return to what existed before. And a politically reunified Germany, leaving aside the question of the borders of 1937, is something I don't consider desirable. Even if it weren't a threat, it would be seen as one, and would accordingly subject us to pressure and vigilance.

But if we speak of a confederation in the center of Europe, a confederation within a federated Europe, I see this model as having a future. A federated relationship between the two German states would also make possible a relationship to Austria, for example, that would alter nothing in Austria's status quo. Maybe we'll eventually come around to saying, "Well, the Austrians didn't make such a bad choice after all with their State Treaty.[3] Perhaps we should try something along those lines—better late than never." I'm not afraid of the word Finlandization—I have tremendous respect for the Finnish people, and I think it's pretty shabby that in the FRG, of all countries, people use the word pejoratively, as a term of contempt. This little country, with its very long border with the Soviet Union, has preserved its independence and demonstrates daily a kind of democracy that certain democrats in the Federal Republic could take a lesson from. In other words: I think we have to begin with the old proposals—from the Rapacki Plan to the Palme Plan—for a nuclear-free Europe,[4] proposals that can always be enlarged, and work out a solution for Germany. Such a solution, in my opinion, should be based on the cultural concept of nationhood, which will not require political unity. This concept, in the spirit of Egon Bahr's "change through rapprochement," would permit the federation of two German states, each of which now has a history of its own, a history we can't simply erase, brief though it is. And their other, longer history could also provide a basis for their relationship.

3. The Austrian *Staatsvertrag,* signed with the Soviet Union in 1955, commits Austria to military neutrality.
4. In 1957 Polish minister of foreign affairs Adam Rapacki presented a plan to the UN General Assembly calling for an atom-bomb-free zone in Europe. In 1980 Swedish prime minister Olaf Palme established a commission that worked for European disarmament.

HEYM: What you propose is certainly worth discussing, and we shouldn't let this dialogue break off—it should be continued in a different place, and not necessarily only by writers.

The funny thing is that these days writers in West Germany, just like us in East Germany, are being called upon to represent some position, to become role models, which is precisely what we don't want. What do we do, after all? We write novels, and I hope those novels are considered good. But we have no right to pose as anything more than ordinary citizens—and yet we're constantly called upon to do that. I wish the politicians, who are actually paid for this, would relieve us of the job of thinking through new developments. I wish they would take up the basic issues for a change, and speak about them in public, too. Not that we writers should withdraw from public life, but people shouldn't expect more of us than we can deliver. . . .

GRASS: And there's another factor. It sounds as though this idea I've expressed so often now is my own, when in fact I see myself as part of a tradition; I see us both as part of a tradition. The German writers of the Enlightenment ended up in opposition to their local rulers not just for reasons of the Enlightenment, but also as patriots. The enlightened patriotic definition of Germany had to do with culture and a unity that contradicted the local rulers' desire for separatism. The tradition persisted from Lessing to Heine and even to Biermann. I used to visit him occasionally while he still lived on Chausseestrasse, and he struck me as a direct descendant in precisely this respect.[5] The same thing happened to me during those discussions we had in East Berlin in the seventies. Every six or eight weeks a few writers from West Berlin would go over, and we would meet our East Berlin counterparts in the apartments of various people, read manuscripts to one another, and discuss, among other things, the differences in the way lyric poetry was evolving in the two German states, and what came across from the manuscripts — or didn't come across, as the case might be. Some of the criticism was pretty harsh.

It's certainly true that we have no mandate to function as spokesmen on political matters. But it's also true that as writers in Germany we've had experiences — and it was always the writers who were driven out of the country first. They would predict bad developments very early on, but no one ever listened to them. . . .

And maybe I could correct one small point. Because of the division of Europe, we like to talk about Western and Eastern Europe. And usually, when we talk about Europe, we mean only Western Europe and have no idea — I think — how bitter that makes people in Czechoslovakia, Hungary, Poland.

HEYM: And the Soviet Union.

---

5. Wolf Biermann, author and singer of political ballads, lived on Chausseestrasse in East Berlin. He was banned from publishing in the GDR and eventually expatriated.

GRASS: And the Soviet Union, of course. That's Europe too, and belongs. And in Prague people don't think of themselves as being in Eastern Europe, but in Central Europe. Maybe that needs to be said in a city like Brussels.

GERMANY—TWO STATES, ONE NATION?

(1 9 7 0)

The title of my lecture is a question, "Germany—two states, one nation?" and I'd like you to take it as a given that the question of nationhood in Germany is older than the history of the two states of the German nation. German history, as far back as we can trace it, has always had a hard time putting the concepts of "Fatherland" or "Nation" or the "German State" in concrete terms.

Since I don't plan to perform a historical crabwalk, which would mean beginning with the Holy Roman Empire of the German Nation, and also because my lecture would be a crashing bore if I set out to portray the history of German separatism as an absurdist cabinet of distorting mirrors, I must be content to refer you to my speech "The Communicating Plural," which I delivered in May 1967 before the Bonn Press Club.

Speech delivered at a seminar sponsored by the Friedrich Ebert Foundation in Bergneustadt, May 23, 1970, and first published in *Die Neue Gesellschaft* (Bonn), July/August 1970.

At the time I wanted to show how inept the Germans have been at defining themselves as a nation, and how convulsively they succumbed to nationalism when they finally imposed nationhood on themselves in the form of a myth that was nothing more than a cult of tyranny. At the time I wanted to show that the federal structure of Germany, with its tendency toward separatism, should serve as the basis for all attempts to endow the idea of the German nation with a new content that would not depend on myth. I saw the two states of the German nation as possibly existing in a confederative relationship. I made a distinction between German unity and a German accord. German unity, history teaches us, causes local crises in the center of Europe to mushroom into supraregional conflicts involving much of the world. German unity has so often proved a threat to our neighbors that we cannot expect them to put up with it anymore—not even as a theoretical goal. On the other hand, a German accord can be worked out, provided it refrains from positing unity. Indeed, to go even further, provided it understands that the renunciation of unity is a sine qua non.

The notes for this speech were jotted down in transit: at the SPD party congress in Saarbrücken, then on a trip to Prague, where I was confronted with the sorrows of the Czechoslovak nation.

It became clear to me there that the Czechoslovak peoples, too, in their natural diversity and autonomy, had a crushing unity imposed on them just at the moment when a democratic accord was beginning to coalesce among the Czechs, the Slovaks, and the many minorities.

It is essential to look at Germany from the outside now and then, this self-absorbed country that tends all too easily to view itself as absolute. The Prague Spring, tinged with melancholy, provided a gloss to Gustav Heinemann's comment, "There are troublesome fatherlands. One of them is Germany."

Because the trip back to Berlin by way of Zinnwald and Dresden was punctuated with delays dictated by bureaucratic precision, it afforded me ample opportunity to ask questions of citizens of the GDR, some in uniform, some not. . . .

My travel impressions, gathered in Saarbrücken at flood stage, among Whitsuntide tourists in Prague, and between Zinnwald and Berlin, conveyed a picture of a moderately troubled and only subliminally hopeful nation. It often seemed to me as though a leaf-green weather frog was being observed from several angles at once, with the observers agreed that neither fine weather nor a downpour was on its way.[1]

Notwithstanding the fact that the opportunities to reduce tension in Central Europe have been very limited over the past twenty years, the Federal Republic's foreign and German policies, especially under Konrad Adenauer, seemed to be based on the impossible. The vague promise of reuniting the German Reich within the borders of 1937 allowed such excessive hubris, expectations, and illusions to accumulate, that any future policy to reduce tension, includ-

---

1. The tree frog, sometimes kept in a glass with a little ladder and used to forecast weather, is colloquially known as a "weather frog" in German, and the term is sometimes applied to a meteorologist on radio or television.

ing the policy presently practiced by the Brandt-Scheel government, can prove successful only when the term "politics of renunciation" no longer stirs people up.[2]

Our task is to eliminate from the catalog of political impossibilities this demand for reunification within the borders of 1937. Now that even the Christian Democrats say only in private what Adenauer often verbalized, the real difficulties begin—with the call for a territorially more modest yet still impossible reunification of the two German states that took shape after 1949, separate and mutually exclusive states.

There can be no unification of the GDR and the Federal Republic on West German terms; there can be no unification of the GDR and the Federal Republic on East German terms. What blocks such a unification—such a concentration of power—is not only the objections of our neighbors in Eastern and Western Europe, but also the fact that these two social systems are mutually exclusive.

And even if the capitalist society in the West were to evolve, under long-term social democratic rule, toward increasing codetermination, the western brand of democratically codeterminative socialism would find itself irreconcilably at odds with the non-democratically controlled state capitalism of eastern socialism. It is easier to picture economic and technical accommodation between traditional private capitalism and traditional state capitalism than accommodation between social democracy and communism.

---

2. *Verzichtpolitik* denotes a willingness to renounce all claims to the territories lost after World War II.

Two years ago in Czechoslovakia, when a first attempt was belatedly made to give centralized communism a democratic basis and legitimation, the invasion by the five Warsaw Pact powers and the Soviet Union's assertion of its power revealed the limits of communism's self-definition. Centralized communism, as conceived by Lenin and consistently developed by Stalin, permits no democratization—unless it begins to question its own dogma, which means also its own power.

In other words, when we speak today of two German states of the German nation, we have to recognize not only the territorial and political division, but also the incompatibility of two existing German social realities.

Shouldn't official recognition and therefore the normal relationship of one foreign country vis-à-vis another be the logical outcome of such considerations? This would seem to make sense. And why do we Germans even need a dangerous term like nation anymore, when our nation is divided territorially, politically, and socially?

I believe that the traditional form of official recognition—meaning a transformation of the divided nation into two foreign countries—will only exacerbate the crisis in Central Europe, by perpetuating the conflict between the power blocs that results from an obsolete fixation on the nation-state. It will double German nationalism and pull the rug out from under the policy of détente in Europe, because two nationalisms will produce twice the unrest, twice the demands for unification, and a permanent crisis in the center of Europe. Official recognition of the GDR, with its implied acceptance of two sovereign states confronting each other, could lead to the Vietnamization of Germany. We hope that the reasonableness and the interests of the neighboring peoples will prevent such a thing from happening. We do not need another Korea or Vietnam.

Instead, let the two German states, with their differences and contrasts, confer a new meaning on the old concept of nationhood by overcoming the traditional conflict-ridden notion. To be sure, the new concept of a nation and its growth depends on the solution of problems that were unknown to the old kind of nation, now destroyed and never to be restored.

In his twenty-point program the federal chancellor outlined problems that can be tackled right now, and solved only by both German states. I want to try to sketch out several other problems, tasks that point toward the future and may sound utopian today.

The first task I would set the two states of the German nation is a thorough inquiry into their recent past. The GDR and the Federal Republic are the successor states of the Third Reich; neither of the two states can bluff its way out of that, for the consequences are binding on both. When Willy Brandt and Willi Stoph, as representatives of their respective states, visited both the site of the Buchenwald concentration camp near Erfurt and a monument to anti-fascism in Kassel, it meant far more than the usual political ritual, because both politicians were obliged to acknowledge German history—a continuing obligation. If this new nation wants to have a clear understanding of itself, it must carry the bankruptcy of the old nation on both shoulders.

The second task I would set the two states of the German nation I will call responsible cooperation: to promote détente in Europe and give concrete form to the previously empty phrase "peaceful coexistence." The Federal Republic and the GDR, as partners in the North Atlantic Alliance and the Warsaw Pact, have duties on their doorstep, European duties. The desirability of gradually disarming the two blocs has been much discussed. The two German states could set an example, and thus give meaning to the new concept of nationhood.

A third task, resulting from the foregoing, would be the cooperation of the two states in the area of peace and conflict research. Where if not in Germany does one have sufficient reason, where if not in Berlin does one have the ideal place to test and develop this new discipline in an environment of perennial conflict, especially since up to now the communist and the democratic perspectives have ascribed different and even contradictory meanings to war and peace?

A fourth task for the two German states of the German nation would be cooperation in providing aid to the countries of the Third World. The Federal Republic and the GDR are industrialized states; so they have an obligation, like all the other industrialized states, to pursue a policy of development that rejects the neocolonialist power politics of the old blocs. When the Federal Republic and the GDR begin to carry out jointly designed development projects— whether in Africa or South America—the concept of "two states of the German nation" will have transcended old-style nationalism and emerged as a model that can help other divided nations resolve their own conflicts. . . .

I have a nightmare vision of a postwar generation that grows up in the traditional straitjacket of nation-statehood simply because the new idea of the two states of the German nation fails to reach the public. Even when I try to explain to my twelve-year-old sons how the old nationalism continues to make its presence felt, and how important it is to see our German nation as an entity with specific tasks to perform in the areas of society, economic development, and peace-keeping, I realize how great the national vacuum is, and how quickly it might be filled again by the demagogues who are always waiting in the wings. The nationalist stew of yore may have gone sour, but it still finds takers.

Education, therefore, should be given top priority, and I would like to stress its importance before this group.

The situation in the other German state is far more troublesome, because it is far more rigid. The GDR had to undergo a rapid, almost seamless transition from National Socialism to Stalinism without the slightest opportunity for establishing a democratic image of itself. Just as the Federal Republic under Adenauer dedicated itself to the principles of separatism and autonomous statehood, the East German Communist Party imposed a restoration of the nation-state modeled on Prussia, which at least made sense in geographical terms. So it's hardly surprising that neighboring Poland took the GDR for the successor state to Prussia.

The Federal Republic's claim to be the only legal representative of Germany and that useless and costly instrument, the Hallstein Doctrine,[3] did much to perpetuate and exacerbate the GDR's sense of injury at not being recognized. No one should be astonished when the GDR expresses its desire for official recognition with such childish vehemence, seemingly deaf to any arguments. Nor did this insistence on recognition, in combination with the country's relative economic strength, win sympathy for the GDR within the Eastern Bloc. Units of the National People's Army took part in an occupation of Czechoslovakia that awakened memories not only in that country but in the other Warsaw Pact powers as well. Memories for which all Germans bear responsibility.

Well fed but in strangely ill-fitting clothes, clothes stylishly tailored on one side, old-fashioned on the other, the two states of the German nation confront each other—awkwardly, because subconsciously they sense how domineering their movements appear to their neighbors, who have reason to be nervous.

In the past year, progress in democratic thinking has at least begun to help the Federal Republic work toward a new understanding of itself and of its political obligations in the center of Europe. Since Gustav Heinemann became president and since Willy Brandt as chancellor has been setting the political course, people abroad—more than in the country itself—have credited the Federal Republic with greater

3. The Hallstein Doctrine, formulated in the fifties by Walter Hallstein, a senior official in the foreign ministry under Adenauer, stated that official recognition of the GDR by other countries would be construed as an unfriendly act toward the FRG.

democratic maturity. The terms so long applied to us — the German thirst for revenge, militarism, neo-Nazism — are losing their credibility.

Yet this positive change in the overall image of the Federal Republic has not yet proved transferable to the GDR, where it might alleviate the old obsessions. Fear of the social democratic alternative is such an integral part of Stalinist communism that any hint of change is strenuously resisted — because each change in the status quo displaces a dogma whose validity depends on things staying as they are.

Since the social-liberal coalition government in the Federal Republic adopted its new policy toward Germany and the East, and ever since the concept of "two states of the German nation" was proclaimed, even though politically it still lacks substance, there has been much talk about a "stony path," a "dry stretch," a "difficult task for the coming decade." The people who issue such cautions are not exaggerating. History does not make leaps. When it does try leaping, it quickly falls back: progress goes a step at a time.

I have tried to point out the difficulties and the contradictions. But my attempt to view the concept of "two states of the German nation" from a different perspective would remain narrow, and trapped in German esotericism, if I failed, in concluding, to call the whole thing into question by alluding, however briefly, to world politics and the current trends, which seem utterly irrational.

In terms of foreign or domestic policy, the United States of America and the Soviet Union are no longer in a position, ideologically or morally, to play the role of custodians of order or world policemen within their spheres of influence.

Having too many far-flung interests and responsibilities creates cracks in the confidence of the two major powers. They become frazzled, touchy, occasionally faint-hearted, then strident. The role of the People's Republic of China was not foreseen in the drama they are acting out. We do not know, and can hardly dictate, the part reason will play in world politics in the future. The contribution we can make, by which I mean the tasks now before the two states of the German nation, should from here on be always on the side of reason, reason in the sense of the European Enlightenment—precisely because Germany has time and again been the bridal bower of irrationality. Unless of course we reject this fine European tradition and mindlessly follow the oracular sayings of our political weather frogs.

THE COMMUNICATING
PLURAL

Speech before the Bonn Press Club

(1 9 6 7)

Ladies and Gentlemen,

More than a month ago, at well-organized *pompes fu-
nèbres,* history was conjured up in this land: Konrad Adenauer's final farewell to his supporters and opponents offered
an occasion for placing a milepost, a milepost that only the
fond and foolish think will never be dislodged. How did *Die
Welt* put it? "The chancellor is dead. A myth is born."

We know this kind of birth announcement. The German people likes its history presented as colossal fate on the
wide screen. From the Battle of the Teutoburg Forest to the
penitential pilgrimage to Canossa and on to the falsification
of the events of June 17, 1953, we are rich in bombastic
disasters. They form a thick sediment of dates in our schoolbooks. So long as we know when the Thirty Years' War
began and when it ended, all is well. Friedrich Schiller tells

Delivered May 29, 1967, under the title "Should the Germans Form One Nation?"
First published in *Süddeutsche Zeitung* (Munich), May 29, 1967.

us all about Wallenstein; and just to make sure we form the right associations, German television broadcasts a *Wallenstein* performance the day after Adenauer's death: history even a child can grasp. The ravens on duty over the Kyffhäuser. The Old Man in the Sachsenwald. They light Hindenburg lamps for us, which are supposed to function as reunification candles, stifling debate and raising morale.[1]

Influenced by such stagecraft, the citizen may well picture history as a broad and mighty stream. Today it is my pleasure to swim against the current of that stream. I call my talk "The Communicating Plural."

I want to challenge a host of firmly entrenched answers by raising the question of nationhood. I want to express the self-evident, even if the self-evident should sound, to some ears, revolutionary. . . .

The nation issue, then. Do the Germans make a nation? Should they make a nation?

As usual, we have trouble with our terminology. For instance: what do we really mean by reunification? Who should be reunited with whom, and under what political conditions? Does reunification mean restoration of the German Reich in the borders of 1937?

There are still sleazy politicians around who foster this sort of hubris. For over a decade, and actually to this day, every German whose vote was desired was promised reuni-

---

1. The ravens on duty refer to the legend of Emperor Friedrich Barbarossa, who was supposed to be buried in the Kyffhäuser Mountain. The "old man in the Sachsenwald" is the Iron Chancellor, Otto von Bismarck. Adenauer was also referred to as "the old man." Paul von Hindenburg, president during the Weimar Republic, allowed himself to be maneuvered into appointing Hitler chancellor.

fication in peace and freedom. Nota bene: in the borders of 1937, and in peace and freedom.

Absurd as it may sound, this flurry of political counterfeiting was accepted by the voter as legal tender. We were ruled without interruption by a party that even today cannot tell us plainly and directly what reunification means, who is to be reunited with whom, and under what political conditions, and how to evaluate the factors that resulted in the dismantling of the Reich, the shrinking of the Reich's territory, and the division of what remained. Instead we were offered crude anti-Communism, with a talent for headlines that reduced Konrad Adenauer's poverty of expression to the level of nineteenth-century German Francophobia. The Russians were to blame for everything. For all other problems the magic word reunification served as a stopgap.

Yet the word can be understood quite differently. At the time of the Holy Roman Empire of the German Nation, the Germans could point to a unity of the Reich, though it was a mystical, not a political, unity. Then, from the beginning of the religious struggles in the sixteenth century, or at least from the conclusion of the Peace of Westphalia, the Roman Empire of the German Nation was divided into two religious and hence also political camps. Yes, at first Protestantism was an issue for all Germans, but Protestantism could never be an issue for an emperor who at the same time was king of Spain. The Counter Reformation won out in the south and west of the empire; the north and east remained Protestant, except for regional pockets. The Main boundary remains politically significant: the three-hundred-year-old antagonisms between Bavaria and Schleswig-Holstein go deeper than the recent ideologically based antagonism between Mecklenburg and Lower Saxony. Yet we should not forget that the division we confront today was in the making long before 1945. From the vantage point of the Rhineland, there was always an East Elbia. East of the Elbe, people said (and still say), things were (and still are) Prussian, Protestant, and thus pagan, in short, communist. The war caused by us and the subsequent cold war, which both Germanys knew how to wage well below the freezing point, transformed the East Elbian border in people's minds into a fortified wall between the two states. It seemed truly grotesque when Konrad Adenauer, a confirmed West Elbian, though he had achieved his highest aspiration by forging a separate Federal Republic, nevertheless spoke of "reunification in peace and freedom." His death made the bankruptcy of his policy visible: reunification is a word devoid of meaning, and we must eliminate it if we wish to keep our credibility.

But what do we put in its place?

New traps for voters, new counterfeits?

Is the House of Springer to extract its new all-German doctrines of salvation from the conjunction of Mars and Uranus, from a favorable double sextile of Jupiter and the sun with Venus and Mercury?

We are familiar with this department-store catalog, in which the same dreary old items are dusted off and presented in new displays. We are encouraged to hope for the collapse of the communist system, if not tomorrow, then the day after tomorrow. Even China has to become a villain in the name of reunification. And every few years, for our all-German constipation, we are given a Europe-enema.

Allow me to outline what is possible and what impossible in the way of a German nation. Because a gap has formed between our tendency toward fragmentation into small states and our tendency toward nationalist hubris. The time has come to put things bluntly.

First of all: anyone who speaks of Germany today must know that in this century two Germanys — first the Kaiser's Germany, then National Socialist Germany — began world wars and lost them. . . .

Furthermore: our inability to learn from a lost war, even to realize that we lost the first and also the second war for very good reasons, accounts for our inept, irrational policies in the aftermath. This ignorance is summed up in what has become a popular expression: We don't want to acknowledge.

The acknowledgment of our guilt has been reduced to irrelevant, belated, ritual expressions. We have lost the bigger picture. We fiddle with a policy that was wrong from the outset. . . .

What has to happen in this country before political conclusions can be drawn from political givens?

Have we lacked good advice, sound counsel?

The advice has been given repeatedly, yet in vain. Let me quote you a passage from the last chapter of Golo Mann's *History of Germany Since 1789.* The chapter is titled, significantly, "Les Allemagnes," the Germanys. Here Mann compares the two Germanys:

[The GDR] officialdom sees the GDR as a new state. Although it makes clumsy, sentimental attempts to establish links with certain episodes in German and Prussian history, it regards the German Reich as dissolved, and must do so because otherwise its state would have no legal basis. Therefore it is very ready to recognize the Federal Republic; it advocates the theory of "two German states." The Federal Republic does not do this. It is not prepared to recognize the GDR and regards itself as the representative of the German Reich which exists *de jure* and must be restored *de facto*.

What has happened since 1949 has led West Germany away from rather than towards this theoretical standpoint; the Federal Republic has developed a strong identity which is not that of the Reich. The focal point of its foreign policy is not the whole of Germany but the Rhineland and southern Germany. An all-German foreign policy would have necessitated an Eastern policy, and the Federal Republic had no such policy.[2]

In this year of 1967 *we* can say that the politics of strength led to the Soviet zone's consolidation in the form of the state known as the GDR. The Federal Republic's claim to be the sole legitimate representative of the German people,

2. Golo Mann, *The History of Germany Since 1789,* trans. Marian Jackson (New York, Washington: Praeger, 1968), p. 532.

or the fiction that it is the legitimate successor to the "Reich" within the borders of 1937, simply demonstrates the schizoid nature of this policy, a policy that claims to be all-German but in reality pursues separateness. The policy of "all or nothing" has permitted us to harvest the nothing without losing face.

Yet the initial situation of divided Germany after the capitulation was not unfavorable. After the cancellation of the Morgenthau Plan, after the ebbing of Stalinism, both parts of Germany had several opportunities to take responsibility for the consequences of the lost war, working together or in tandem, and to win back the trust of their neighbors, who had been their enemies. Both Germanys frittered away the capital the victors had invested in them; one Germany revived Stalinism and isolated itself, while the Federal Republic had an even better opportunity and failed to seize it: all the mileposts of the Adenauer era, from rearmament to the Hallstein Doctrine, violated the preamble of the Basic Law. Thus both provisional states were consolidated, and today we have two Germanys. The fact that our people have grown accustomed to this situation and at the same time react to it hysterically proves that we Germans are in no condition to form one nation.

For the structure of the two German states is naturally federative. In both states this federative structure is confirmed by law. Article 1 of the GDR's constitution still reads: "Germany is an indivisible democratic republic; it rests upon the individual provinces, the *Länder* . . ." But this federalism has been able to express itself fully only in the Federal

Republic; the GDR presents a unified Prussian face and tries to blur the existing differences, for instance between Mecklenburg and Saxony. Yet federalism—meaning the legal relationship of separate parts *to* each other, *with* each other, and, in the civic sense, *for* each other, offers the only suitable basis for the two German states. Until now, they have lived only *against* each other. And so the tradition of dualism has been carried to the point of division.

Only seldom, and then under duress, has Germany been a unified national bloc overriding the control of its individual provinces. On the other hand, German history teaches us that the federal structure of our country has repeatedly, and to this day, driven us to separatism. At the time of the French Revolution, while France was pioneering the nation-state, one thousand seven hundred eighty-nine German territorial entities were plying their absolutist small trade. Even Napoleon's project, the simplification of the German map, entailed the establishment of thirty-six separate states within the German confederation after the Congress of Vienna. It took the Prussians and their extreme methods to achieve unity, with results that are well known and likewise extreme. We never mastered moderation. So between nationalism and separatism lies the only real possibility for us, seldom tried: confederation, that is, an economically sound and politically and culturally flexible linkage of the provinces. It could be a *patria* for us; but already, again, the image begins to blur. . . .

Since this new German separatism in the form of two states has been making two completely separate histories, a generation has grown up seeing itself as citizens of the Federal Republic on the one hand, and of the GDR on the other. Citizens who do not know much about each other. Two different educational systems have intentionally educated this generation away from each other. During the fifties the mutual alienation of the two German-speaking states became so rigid and ideological that in the Federal Republic people, to the question, "Is Walter Ulbricht a German?" answered without hesitation, "No!" Non-Germans in both East and West say, with good reason, "Why shouldn't there be two states, if the Germans themselves are so determined to have it that way?"

In this connection I'd like to mention an essay by Arnulf Baring that appeared in August 1962 and remains pertinent today: "Patriotic Question Marks." The essay ends with a provocation in the form of a paradox: "Any rapprochement in Germany is predicated on the recognition of its division!"

Let me expand on that. A confederated Germany is thinkable only in conjunction with the recognition of the facts — that is, the lost war which we must pay for, its consequences, and the federative nature of the two states. It will take patience and political clearheadedness to bring about such a confederation. It will take the recognition, at long last, of the Oder-Neisse border, which recognition should be declared an advance concession toward a peace treaty.

In both German states the prerequisites are still lacking for the achievement of this goal. Neither the GDR's Prussian-Stalinist concept of the state nor the Federal Republic's half-confessed nostalgia for the old Confederation of the Rhine[3] is a suitable starting point for the confederation of the two German states. A nightmare is already in the making, and, like many German nightmares, it carries the threat of becoming reality: it does not seem so unlikely that in the seventies the strong Prussian-Stalinist wing in the GDR may reach an accord with the increasingly powerful nationalist-conservative wing in the Federal Republic—at the expense of liberal federalism, of social democracy. German nationalists on the right, together with rightist Stalinists, could give birth to a monstrosity of a nation. We can only hope that this will be prevented by the Germans' growing insight into themselves.

We must learn to see that there is no inherent positive value in the idea of nationhood.

We must recognize that the French nation rests on historical givens that we lack. Switzerland, on the other hand, is an example of a confederation that does not preclude a sense of nationhood.

In spite of all the ideological rigidity on both sides of the border, and without the usual envious staring at other models—whose centralized structure should be a warning to us—we should pursue instead a policy that makes regression to the notion of a nation-state impossible. A policy that avoids the empty word reunification and attempts, rather, a gradual rapprochement, whose goal would be a confederation of two German provincial alliances.

3. A league of German principalities formed in 1806 under the protection of Napoleon; its members included Bavaria, Württemberg, Saxony, Westphalia, and Baden.

On May 6, 1947 the first and last postwar conference of all the German prime ministers took place in Munich, chaired by Ludwig Erhard, then prime minister of Bavaria. That same day a conflict arose over the agenda, and the five provincial heads from the Soviet zone walked out. If a policy of rapprochement is to be reinstituted twenty years later, it will be important to remember that failed conference of May 1947 and the reasons for its failure. At the same time, the Bundestag and Volkskammer delegates should be mindful that both the GDR constitution that was finally adopted and our Emergency Decrees[4] are new evidence of separatist tendencies.

Here is my thesis: since our fundamental disposition indicates that we are not suited to forming a nation-state, since experience has taught us—and our cultural multiplicity confirms—that we should not form a nation-state, we must recognize federalism as our best chance and last chance. Neither as one nation nor as two in conflict can we guarantee our neighbors to the east and the west any security. Poland and Czechoslovakia would find a federalized GDR far less sinister as a neighbor than the present GDR, centralized successor to the Prussian state.

And the Federal Republic would have to recognize the

4. The Emergency Decrees, promulgated in May 1968 by a two-thirds majority of the Bundestag and unanimously approved by the provincial legislatures after many years of heated debate, were violently opposed by student and worker groups, in particular during the period of political and domestic unrest that followed the student uprisings of 1967. The decrees were seen as severely limiting certain civil-rights provisions of the Basic Law, in the name of "law and order" and "national security."

other state officially and relinquish its claim to be the sole representative of the German people. At the same time it would have to urge the GDR to provide constitutional guarantees of the hegemony of its individual provinces. This would be a precondition for federal cooperation among the ten provinces of the Federal Republic, including the province of Berlin, and the five provinces of the GDR. In this confederation of two states, provinces with Christian democratic, social democratic, and communist governments will have to work together. In Italy and France people take for granted the often cacophonous concert of opposing parties; the same thing should become routinely accepted among the Germans. Political opponents who until now unconditionally excluded each other will have to get used to holding talks. The deliberative body of this confederation might meet alternately in Leipzig and Frankfurt/Main. It will have no lack of tasks before it. One will be to disarm two standing armies, a step at a time. Another will be to finance joint research projects and economic development projects with the monies that are thus freed up. Another will be to eliminate the political penal system in both confederated states. Another will be to institute joint negotiations directed toward a peace treaty.

It is imperative that a beginning be made; time is not on our side. We should be able to persuade our western and eastern neighbors of the desirability of this confederation of two federal German states, especially as such a rapprochement does not mean reunification but instead will promote détente between East and West and contribute to a future European solution, which will certainly be federal in character.

Unity, both European and German, does not depend on political unification. Germany has been unified only under duress, and always to its own detriment. Unification is an idea that runs counter to human nature; it restricts freedom. Whereas unity means a free decision made by many. The German nation should come to mean the coexistence, in harmony and collaboration, of the Bavarians and Saxons, the Swabians and Thuringians, the Westphalians and the Mecklenburgers. Germany in the singular is a calculation that will never balance; as a sum, it is a communicating plural.

I have had the temerity to speak of these things to you, German reporters long familiar with the fictions as well as with the real possibilities of national policy. It may be that in the ensuing discussion a bag of facts will be emptied; then each person can call out his favorite facts. We have come to rely on the safety of facts to support our various positions—in the absence of a general agreement as to who and what we are. Though I, too, by now greet misunderstandings and even willful misinterpretations as old acquaintances, I would still like to ask you to reexamine your own views, to reexamine them, no matter how many facts you as reporters have at your fingertips, in the larger context of the German lack of self-awareness.

We don't know whether it was Goethe or Schiller who said this, but let me quote in closing—for Mannheim and Jena, for Weimar and Frankfurt—the following couplet from the "Xenien":

GERMAN NATIONAL CHARACTER

To form yourselves into a nation, Germans,
  you hope in vain;
Form yourselves, rather, as well you can,
  into freer beings.[5]

5. In the *Musenalmanach für das Jahr 1797*, Goethe and Schiller published a series of "Xenien," satirical distichs on contemporary literature and politics.

WHAT IS THE GERMAN'S FATHERLAND?

(1 9 6 5)

"What Is the German's Fatherland?" is the title of my speech, and it also is the beginning of a poem that I'd like to share with you:

> What is the German's fatherland?
> Is it the Prussian's land, the Saxon's land?
> Is it on the Rhine, where the vineyards bloom?
> Is it on the Belt, where the seagulls swoop?
> Oh, no! no! no!
> His fatherland needs greater scope!
>
> What is the German's fatherland?
> Is it the Bavarian's land or Styrian's land?
> Is it where the Marsian's livestock grazes?
> Or where their iron the Mark folk raises?
> Oh, no! no! no!
> His fatherland needs greater scope!

Speech for the national election campaign of 1965, first published separately under the same title (Neuwied and Berlin: Luchterhand, 1965).

What Is the German's Fatherland?

What is the German's fatherland?
Is it the Pomeranian's land, the Westphalian's land?
Is it where the sands of the north dunes blow?
Is it where the Danube's waters flow?
Oh, no! no! no!
His fatherland needs greater scope!

What is the German's fatherland?
Come, name for me this mighty land!
Is it the land of the Swiss or of the Tyrol?
Such a land and people would please me well.
But no! no! no!
His fatherland needs greater scope!

What is the German's fatherland?
Come, name for me this mighty land!
It must be Austria, no doubt,
So rich in honor and victorious rout?
Oh, no! no! no!
His fatherland needs greater scope!

What is the German's fatherland?
Come, name for me this mighty land!
As far as the German tongue resounds
And from God in heaven song abounds:
There it must be!
That, noble German, belongs to thee!

That is the German's fatherland,
Where an oath is the touch of hand to hand,

Where loyalty from a man's eye does dart,
And love resides in every heart—
There it must be!
That, noble German, belongs to thee!

That is the German's fatherland,
Where the glitter of foreign lands is scorned,
Where every Frenchman is a bitter foe,
And every German a friend we know,
There it must be!
Let the whole of Germany belong to thee!

Let the whole of Germany belong to thee!
Oh, God in Heaven, our guardian be,
And fill our hearts with German valor,
That we may love it in goodness and honor.
There it must be!
Let the whole of Germany belong to thee!

Despite appearances, this hymn was not cooked up in the Ministry for All-German Affairs; the poet was called Ernst Moritz Arndt, and a statue of him stands in Bonn.[1] When I was in school, I had to learn this unique thing by heart. I certainly hope the memory banks of our newest voters are not being clogged with such multi-stanzaic nonsense. Though if they read Karl May's *Blue-red Methusalem,*[2] in the last chap-

1. Ernst Moritz Arndt (1769–1860) was a prolific writer whose German nationalism was sparked by opposition to Napoleon.
2. Karl May (1842–1912) was a best-selling author of travel and adventure stories for young people. Most are set among the American Indians or desert Arabs.

ter they will find a merry gathering of men in their cups who tell us, in several-part harmony, what the German's fatherland is. But with the help of this song and the scene from Karl May we can imagine what a satisfying tidbit this poem must have been at merry songfests, graduation parties, and other occasions, from Wilhelm's times to Adolf's, and how it fed nationalist hubris. But we do Ernst Moritz Arndt an injustice if we blame him for the subsequent perversion of his song, which was written out of the enthusiasm left over from the Wars of Liberation. And I am grateful to this literary colleague, who lent his name to so many German secondary schools, for posing the question so intriguingly. What is the German's fatherland? . . .

I am afraid I will disappoint anyone who thinks that after such a running start I mean to come up immediately with proposals for reunification, or that I know how to fulfill Konrad Adenauer's campaign promise to the refugees from the East: "You'll all get back to your old homes!"

Since 1955, when the Treaty on Germany was signed, and during our Wall-building period, the government of the Federal Republic has proved successful in perpetuating Germany's division, to the short-term advantage of the FRG and the lasting detriment of our fellow countrymen in the GDR. As far as those provinces are concerned to which Ernst Moritz Arndt alludes indirectly — Silesia, Eastern Pomerania, East Prussia — I, who come from those parts, can only gnash my teeth and beat my breast, and speak the truth: We let those provinces slip through our fingers; we gambled them away; we lost them in taking on the world. Ernst Moritz Arndt's poem "What is the German's Fatherland?" has become shorter. Though not so short that we have to be worried. Perhaps the next government of the Federal Republic will include realistic-minded politicians who will know how to conduct negotiations based on a peace treaty, because the Allies disagreed at Potsdam and Yalta on the fate of Stettin and the Lausitz Point.

On Sundays Seebohm bellows his claims to the Sudetenland in the ears of a horrified world.[3] My fellow countrymen from Danzig even maintain a shadow senate in Lübeck that for years now has been promising old folks from Danzig and the Werder region that one day the free city of Danzig will exist once more. Lies and cynicism directed at old people who have never managed to feel at home in the West, who have kept that broad, slow speech that is like spreading butter on bread. For years such rhetorical bubbles have taken the place of a constructive foreign policy. Let me say it again: If we really care about Stettin and the Lausitz region, we should find the courage to delete Königsberg and Breslau, Kolberg and Schneidemühl as geographical entries in our song "What Is the German's Fatherland?" But that doesn't mean we should dissolve the refugee associations and forget those provinces that once were German. By all means, let us put a stop to the expensive refugee rallies where political functionaries grow fatter. In their place I would propose serious research on dying dialects and—I am not afraid of supercilious smiles—the establishment of well-planned, vital

3. Hans-Christof Seebohm was an early and longtime cabinet member, minister of transportation under both Adenauer and Erhard between 1949 and 1966. Before that he was active in politics in Lower Saxony. Beginning in 1959 he was chief spokesman for the Sudeten-German Provincial League.

cities with names like New Königsberg, New Allenstein, New Breslau, New Görlitz, New Kolberg, and New Danzig.

Let us be founders of cities! We have room in the Eifel region, in the Hunsrück area, in the Ems territory, in the Bavarian Forest. We have no lack of underutilized areas that could be developed in this realistic way. I would be glad to do my part toward laying the cornerstone for the city of New Danzig, and it need not be on the Baltic. Do I hear someone saying utopia? Nothing of the sort. Here the question "What is the German's fatherland?" would be answered concretely. It will take good sense and a dose of pioneering spirit — the kind the German emigrants to America displayed when they founded Hamburg, Frankfurt, and Berlin in the Midwest — to recover not lost provinces but the essence of what was once the German's fatherland.

After the war the glassblowers and glass jewelry manufacturers of the city of Gablonz in the Sudetenland provided an example of this pioneering spirit when they founded the city of New Gablonz in southern Germany. Our land is rich enough to risk founding such new cities. I see modern, boldly planned cities going up, and since Germany now has a shortage of universities and other institutions of higher learning, they can become centers of research and scholarship. Architects could try new approaches that would get us out of our urban-planning stalemate. I see traditional industries like those in Breslau, Danzig, and Königsberg becoming established. And perhaps even the dying dialects — Gerhart Hauptmann's Silesian and my beloved Danzig Low German — will experience a renaissance, grotesquely mixed with Frisian and Bavarian accents.

A thousand sociologists shake their heads. Shouts of "Too late!"—"Should have been done ten years ago!"—"He's nuts!" The word *Verzichtpolitiker* rears its ugly head.[4] I see graying Riders to the East drawing those SA daggers that had been carefully oiled and put away: they want to carve me into the usual rootless cosmopolitan, the stereotypical communist. And perhaps the social democrats I cherish so dearly will say "Thanks, but no thanks" to such ammunition. But for me the important thing is to answer that old question of Ernst Moritz Arndt's: "What is the German's fatherland?" I say: Whatever we make of it. Whatever values we place first: the utterances of tank division commander Guderian, or the courageous speech by the social democratic Reichstag deputy Otto Wels.[5] After so many lost wars, after blitzkrieg victories and battles of encirclement, after all the horrors we have been capable of, we should finally let reason, moderation, and our fatherland's real talent triumph—the talent for scholarship, which once flourished and then was increasingly repressed. The choice is ours.

In New York, on May 8, I saw parts of the East Berlin victory parade on American television. The Telstar Early Bird made this possible. I saw the People's Army marching in snappy formation. Shades of Prussia. In Ulbricht's realm a corrupt tradition was being shamelessly preserved. Looking

4. One who believes in the "politics of renunciation."
5. Heinz Guderian was the commander of Hitler's armored divisions and an important military strategist. Otto Wels in March 1933 delivered a speech explaining why all ninety-four social democratic delegates intended to vote against a constitutional change that would allow Hitler's government to rule for four years without the assent of the Reichstag.

fearsome but also comical, like any overinflated power, the army marched past. Altogether a picture that could easily make one forget that this would-be state calls itself the "Peace Camp." O great bearded Marx! What have they done to you there? In what prison would you be locked up today?

Twenty years after the unconditional surrender of a country that called itself Greater Germany, there I was sitting in a New York hotel room, staring at the screen and seeing this same unnatural flailing of the legs that had created the rhythm of my youth. That, too, is the German's fatherland. But is it only that? Anyone who lives in Berlin knows that the majority of our countrymen in the GDR give this Prussian-Stalinist variation on the goose step a wide berth. Last fall I spent a few days in Weimar. Let's not talk about the ridiculous congress held there to keep alive the old popular Marxism. During the intermissions I could take a break from defending Kafka, Joyce, or our "degenerate artists," as Mr. Erhard recently chose to call them, against hidebound functionaries and all-German Philistines. I seized these occasions to look around me.

He who has ears, let him hear. The hour is late. Our countrymen over there, to whom the soapbox orators refer as "our brothers and sisters," are prepared to write us off. They know the score. They listen to western radio stations. The language we use, from "all-German concerns" to the solemn clichés trotted out for the seventeenth of June, including the refrain, "Let the whole of Germany belong to thee," has worn out their ears. Without beating around the bush and with a slightly mocking tone they offer a blunt summary of fourteen years of West German reunification policy. People said to me, "Your Adenauer, he knew perfectly well what he was doing. Reunification wasn't in the cards. That would have meant an all-German social democratic government. Besides, we're not Catholic."

You can take this statement and refine it and add all sorts of qualifiers, and take the ifs and the buts into account, and put the blame on the Allies or on the wicked Russians, just as you please, but anyone who is sick and tired of self-deception, anyone who is willing to take a national inventory, using his head and an accurate memory, and who asks himself the question "What is the German's fatherland?" will soon recognize that the same shouters and crusaders who want to bring the Sudetenland and Gleiwitz home into the Reich have actually been engaged in secretly—and not unskillfully—selling out our fatherland, renouncing all claims to Dresden and Magdeburg, Weimar and Rostock.

Let us look back: on June 16 and 17, 1953 a German workers' uprising occurred in East Berlin and the Soviet occupation zone. In its most powerful moments—when it began on Stalinallee and when it failed—it clearly bore social democratic traits, and caused Walter Ulbricht's dictatorship to totter, if only for a few hours. The GDR government called the workers' uprising a fascist putsch attempt, and the West Germans called it a popular uprising, though it can easily be shown that the bourgeoisie and the peasants, the civil servants and the intellectuals, with a few laudable exceptions, stayed home. It was the German workers who took the initiative, the workers from Henningsdorf, Buna, Leuna, Halle, and Merseburg who took the risk, while we trivialized their desperate, moving, and finally tragic ef-

fort into a national holiday. That, too, is the German's fatherland: a moment of truth that lasted two days, and a lie
that has grown fatter and fatter over the course of twelve
years. Where is the youth, and where is my burned generation, who should know better, where are they, that they
swallowed this lie without a peep? Don't say, "That's news
to us, we knew nothing about it." You readers of *Spiegel*
and *Pardon,* you subscribers to *konkret* and *Civis,* you frater-
nity students and nonfraternity students, don't shrug your
shoulders and say, "What difference does it make whether
it was a workers' uprising or a popular uprising, it didn't
do any good anyway." Our countrymen, who stand ready
to accuse you, will not let you off that easily, because it was
impossible not to have heard—unless a person stuffed his
ears with lottery tickets, vacation plans, and "no experiments." [6]

On July 1, 1953, when the seventeenth of June was des-
ignated the "Day of German Unity," a relatively unknown
Bundestag delegate from Berlin, Willy Brandt, gave a tough
speech. Brandt was the first to warn against falsifying the
workers' uprising. Allow me to quote a rather long passage
from this great speech, which has lost none of its validity.
Brandt said:

> Anyone who still believes that he can call into ques-
> tion the democratic and national integrity of the
> German workers' movement and of German social

6. "No experiments" was the slogan of the CDU during the campaigns of Erhard
and Kurt Georg Kiesinger; it implied that one should not rock the economic and
political boat, as the SPD proposed to do.

democracy thereby becomes responsible for bringing about yet another division in our people.

The illusions in foreign policy in the past few years, the lack of realism can be laid at the door of those who did not include negotiations between East and West in their calculations. I should add that we see a great danger in the fact that the major powers are still not negotiating for a solution to the German Question. German politics must do nothing to increase this danger.

There is no solution other than a peaceful solution to the German Question. There is no possibility for a solution other than through negotiation. We call for more active involvement, more decisiveness in the struggle for German unity in peace and freedom.

Thus spoke the unknown delegate in 1953, and thus speaks the mayor of Berlin, Willy Brandt, to this day. Back then his words fell on deaf ears. Will he be heard today? Back then party politics and fear of the communists put blinders on many. Are we prepared today, from the position of strength our democratic constitution gives us, and now that we are self-confident and mature at last, to meet our political opponent in prolonged, step-by-step negotiations? Or must more decades pass during which the Bundeswehr and the People's Army confront each other, as if such confrontation were the last word in wisdom? The Bundestag elections on September 19 will answer the question of what the German's fatherland is today and will be tomorrow. Our fellow countrymen, from whom Ulbricht still withholds free elections, will be watching us as we vote. I hope that anyone who still hesitates to exercise his right to vote will consider how many of the workers who rose up in June 1953 against injustice and dictatorship would love to vote in his place. Don't pass it up lightly, our hard-earned right to vote!

I outlined this speech in June, in America. There, on various university campuses, at the usual receptions, during discussions in hotel lobbies, wherever I met German emigrants, I found myself thinking about that grotesque school poem we owe to Ernst Moritz Arndt. They, too, the injured and embittered, the quiet ones who lost their power of speech in '33, the shy ones who have forgotten their native tongue over the years, the old professors asking about Heidelberg and Göttingen, the businessmen who still remember Leipzig and Frankfurt with fondness, all of them whom we miss today, inhabit a province without borders, a province that is scattered all over the world, a province that painfully, and often against their will, constitutes the German's fatherland.

In the last few years the German emigrants have often enough had filth thrown at them—if only as a way of smearing Willy Brandt. This filth is provided free of charge by the team of Kapfinger and Strauss[7] to all those interested, including the venerable federal chancellor. If the spiritual province of the German emigrants is not to be lost to our fatherland, too, the citizens of the Federal Republic and

---

7. Hans Kapfinger was an editor and publisher in Passau, Bavaria. His *Bayernkurier* was notorious for propagating extreme right-wing views. Franz Josef Strauss, his crony, was for many years the leading political figure in Bavaria, cofounder of the CSU and its general secretary and then chairman. A staunch opponent of Brandt's *Ostpolitik*.

especially the youth will have to stop the verbal barrage that Joseph Goebbels set in motion. To be talking still about "degenerate art," Mr. Erhard, is a new slap in the face to those painters, writers, and composers who were persecuted and proscribed, who died or survived, who stayed here or emigrated. Paul Klee and Max Beckmann, Alban Berg and Kurt Weill, Alfred Döblin and Else Lasker-Schüler were driven out of this country, Mr. Erhard, by the very formula you parrot, which makes you doubly irreponsible. Even if you are not endowed with insight and artistic sensibility, at least a sense of shame should restrain you from using the language of the National Socialists. With its "execution" and "eradication," with such linguistic monstrosities as "folkish" and "degenerate," that language left us a depressing legacy that should not—should never again—be the German's fatherland.

Let me make one last attempt to answer Ernst Moritz Arndt's question. In New York, getting a sense for that province of German emigrants I'd like to see included in the German's fatherland, I wrote this "Transatlantic Elegy":

> In a mood to smile, with success, my little dog
>   always at my heel.
> On the road in the land of Walt Whitman, with
>   light luggage.
> Swimming unfettered between conferences, carried
>   by the current of talk.
> During breaks, as long as clinking ice cubes speak
>   their mind to glasses,
> it touches you and names its name.

What Is the German's Fatherland?

In New Haven and Cincinnati, questioned
        by emigrants,
who back then, when our intellect emigrated,
could take along nothing but language,
and still spread the multitude of tongues with
Swabian, Saxon, Hessian, good-naturedly stroking
        each word,
in Washington and New York they asked me,
warming their whiskey with their hands:
How does it look over there?
Do people still say——?
And your young people?
Do they know? Do they want to? One hears
        so little.
    Shyness stretched out these questions,
    and they remembered with caution,
    as if to spare someone's feelings:
Should one go back?
Is there still room for the likes of us?
And won't my German——I know it's
        old-fashioned——
Tip people off that I . . . for so long . . .
    And I replied, warming my whiskey:
It's gotten better.
We have a good constitution.
Now, finally, my generation is stirring.
Soon, in September, there'll be elections.
    And when I suffered from lack of words,
    they helped me
    with their emigrated language, still beautiful.

Hear the legend from over there:
    There was a thousand-fold librarian,
    who preserved the literary legacies
    of those whose books had gone up in flames,
        back then.
He smiled conservatively and wished me luck for
    September.

OPEN LETTER TO
ANNA SEGHERS

Berlin, August 14, 1961

To the President
of the German Writers' Union
in the GDR

Dear Frau Anna Seghers:

Yesterday I was startled awake by one of those sudden operations so familiar to us Germans, with tank noises in the background, radio commentary, and the usual Beethoven symphony. When I did not want to believe what the radio was serving up for breakfast, I went to the Friedrichstrasse station, went to the Brandenburg Gate, and found myself face to face with naked power, which nevertheless

First published under the title "And What Can the Writers Do?" in *Die Zeit* (Hamburg), August 18, 1961. Seghers was a novelist who spent the Hitler years in France and Mexico, then returned to East Berlin in 1947 and served until 1978 as president of the Writers' Union.

stank of pigskin. The minute I find myself in danger, I become overanxious, like all once-burned children, and have the tendency to cry for help. I groped around in my head and heart for names, names promising help; and your name, revered Frau Anna Seghers, became the straw I do not want to let go of.

It was you who after that never-to-be-forgotten war taught my generation, or anyone who had ears to hear, to distinguish justice from injustice. Your book *The Seventh Cross* formed me, sharpened my eye, so that I can still recognize a Globke or a Schröder in any disguise, even when they call themselves humanists, Christians, or activists. The anxiety felt by your protagonist, Georg Heisler, communicated itself to me once and for all; except that the commandant of the concentration camp is no longer called Fahrenberg but Walter Ulbricht, and he presides over your state. I am not Klaus Mann, and your spirit is diametrically opposed to the spirit of the fascist Gottfried Benn, and yet, with the presumptuousness of my generation, I refer you to the letter Klaus Mann wrote to Gottfried Benn on May 9, 1933.[1] For you and for myself let me transform those two dead men's ninth of May into our living August 14, 1961. Up to now you have been the epitome of resistance to violence; it is impossible that you should fall prey to the irrationalism of a Gottfried Benn and fail to recognize the violent nature of a dictatorship that has scantily yet cleverly wrapped itself in your

1. Klaus Mann, eldest son of the writer Thoman Mann and a prolific writer himself, sharply rebuked the Expressionist poet Gottfried Benn for supporting Hitler and National Socialism.

dream of socialism and communism, a dream I do not dream but which I respect, as I do any dream. . . .

Please do not tell me to wait for the future, which, as you know, being a writer, is resurrected hourly in the past. Let us stick to today, August 14, 1961. Today nightmares in the form of tanks are parked at Leipziger Strasse, disturbing all sleep and threatening citizens while claiming to protect them. Today it is dangerous to live in your state, and it is impossible to leave your state. . . .

I want to make this day our day. I want you, as a woman at once weak and strong, to arm your voice and speak out against the tanks, against this barbed wire that seems to be perpetually manufactured in Germany, the same barbed wire that once provided the concentration camps with security. . . .

This letter, revered Frau Anna Seghers, must be an "open letter." I am sending you the original by way of the Writers' Union in East Berlin. I am sending a copy to the daily *Neues Deutschland*, asking them to publish it, and a second copy to the weekly *Die Zeit* in Hamburg.[2]

Seeking help, I send you best regards from

Günter Grass

2. The *Neues Deutschland* is the official party organ in East Berlin. *Die Zeit* is a highly respected intellectual weekly newspaper, left of center in its editorial policies.

WRITING AFTER

AUSCHWITZ

(1 9 9 0)

A writer, asked to give an account of himself, which means of his work, would have to evaporate into that ironic distance in which everything shrinks if he wished to avoid discussing the time period that has marked him, shaped him, kept him immobilized in erroneous contradictions (despite various changes of scene), and made him a witness. As I title this lecture "Writing after Auschwitz" and now look for a place to begin, I know I am bound to disappoint. My topic is too demanding. Let the attempt be made, however.

Since I was invited by a university and am speaking specifically to students, thus finding myself face to face with the innocent curiosity of a generation that grew up under conditions entirely different from my own, let me first go back a few decades and sketch the circumstances in which I found myself in May 1945.

When I was seventeen years of age, living with a hundred

Speech given February 13 at the Johann Wolfgang Goethe University in Frankfurt am Main.

thousand others in an American prison camp out under the open sky, in a foxhole, I was famished, and because of this I focused, with the cunning born of hunger, exclusively on survival—otherwise I had not a clear notion in my head. Rendered stupid by dogma and accordingly fixated on lofty goals: this was the state in which the Third Reich released me and many of my generation from our oaths of loyalty. "The flag is superior to death" was one of its life-denying certainties.

All this stupidity resulted not only from a schooling knocked full of holes by the war—when I reached fifteen, my time as Luftwaffe helper began, which I mistakenly welcomed as liberation from school—it was, rather, an over-arching stupidity, one that transcended differences of class and religion, one that was nourished by German compla-cency. Its ideological slogans usually began with "We Ger-mans are . . . ," "To be German means . . . ," and, finally, "A German would never . . ."

This last-quoted rule lasted even beyond the capitulation of the Greater German Reich and took on the stubborn force of incorrigibility. For when I, with many of my gen-eration—leaving aside our fathers and mothers for now—was confronted with the results of the crimes for which Germans were responsible, crimes that would be summed up in the image of Auschwitz, I said: Impossible. I said to myself and to others, and others said to themselves and to me: "Germans would never do a thing like that."

This self-confirming Never was even pleased to view it-self as steadfast. In response to the overwhelming number of photographs showing piles of shoes here, piles of hair there, and again and again bodies piled on top of each other, captioned with numerals I could not grasp and foreign-sounding place names—Treblinka, Sobibor, Auschwitz—there was one ready answer, spoken or unspoken, but always firm, whenever American educational zeal forced us seventeen- and eighteen-year-olds to look at the documentary photos: Germans never could have done, never did do a thing like that.

Even when the Never collapsed (if not earlier, then with the Nuremberg Trials), the former Reich Youth Leader Baldur von Schirach declared that we, the Hitler Youth, were free of responsibility. It took several more years before I began to realize: This will not go away; our shame cannot be repressed or come to terms with. The insistent concreteness of those photographs—the shoes, the glasses, the hair, the corpses—resisted abstraction. Even if surrounded with explanations, Auschwitz can never be grasped.

Since then, much time has passed. Certain historians have been busy digging up facts and figures to make this "unfortunate phase in German history," as they call it, a valid academic subject. Yet no matter what has been admitted to, lamented, or otherwise said out of a sense of guilt—as in this speech—the monstrous phenomenon for which the name Auschwitz stands remains beyond facts and figures, beyond the cushioning academic study, a thing inaccessible to any confession of guilt. Therefore it remains impossible to grasp, forming such a divide in human history that one is tempted to date events before and after Auschwitz.

And in retrospect a persistent question confronts the writer: How was it possible to write—after Auschwitz? Was this question posed merely to fulfill a ritual of contrition? Was the agonized self-searching of the fifties and early sixties no more than a literary exercise? And does the question even matter nowadays, when the very idea of literature is being challenged by the new media?

Back to the stupid, unwavering adolescent. Come to think of it, he wasn't so stupid and unwavering. Because despite the shortness of his schooling he had had a few teachers who taught him, more in secret than openly, aesthetic values, artistic sensibility. The woman sculptor, for example, assigned to teaching as her compulsory wartime service, who noticed the schoolboy constantly drawing and slipped him exhibition catalogs from the twenties. At considerable risk, she shocked and infected him with the work of Kirchner, Lehmbruck, Nolde, Beckmann. I clung to that. Or it clung to me. In the face of such artistic provocations the certainty of this Hitler Youth began to waver, or, rather, it did not waver but softened in one spot, and let in other kinds of egocentric certainties — the unthinking, unfocused, yet intense, bold desire to be an artist.

From the age of twelve, I could not be dissuaded from this — not by the paternal pointing to a more solid profession, not by the difficult times later on: ruins everywhere, and nothing to eat. My youthful obsession kept its vitality, survived unharmed — again, unwaveringly — the end of the war, then the first postwar years, and even the currency reform, which wrought changes all around.

And thus the choice of career was made. After an apprenticeship as a stonemason and sculptor, I went to study sculpture, first at the Academy of Art in Düsseldorf, then at the School of Fine Arts in Berlin. Yet these autobiographical data do not say much, except perhaps that my desire to become an artist showed—you might say an admirable, but I would say, in retrospect, a questionable singleness of purpose: admirable, perhaps, because the decision was made quite simply, despite my parents' reservations and without regard for material security, but still questionable and in the end not admirable at all, because my artistic development, which soon led by way of poetry to writing, again proceeded unwaveringly, not wavering even in the face of Auschwitz.

No, my path was not chosen in ignorance, for in the meantime all the horrors had been brought to light. Nevertheless my path led me blindly, with a purposeful blindness, past Auschwitz. After all, there were plenty of other signposts. Not the sort that blocked one and caused one's step to hesitate. The names of previously unknown authors lured me, seized possession of me: Döblin, Dos Passos, Trakl, Apollinaire. The art exhibitions of those years were not self-stylized displays by bored professionals; instead, they opened up vistas of new worlds—Henry Moore or Chagall in Düsseldorf, Picasso in Hamburg. And travel became possible: hitchhiking to Italy, to see not only the Etruscans but also spare, earth-toned pictures by Morandi.

As the ruins increasingly vanished from view, and though people all around resumed weaving according to the old pattern, it was a time of radical change—and of the illusion that one could build something new on old foundations.

I devoured book after book. Addicted to images, I devoured pictures, drawings, without any plan, obsessed with art and its methods. As a once-burned child, I found it sufficient to oppose — more out of instinct than on the basis of arguments — the first federal chancellor, Konrad Adenauer, the nouveau-riche nonsense of the developing "economic miracle," the hypocritical Christian restoration, and rearmament, of course, and of course Adenauer's secretary of state Globke, his expert in East German intelligence, Gehlen, and other obscene deputies of the master politician from the Rhineland.

I recall Easter marches organized to protest the atom bomb. Always there, always in opposition. The obstinate horror of the seventeen-year-old who had refused to believe the atrocity stories had given way to opposition on general principle. In the meantime the real dimensions of the genocide were now demonstrated in volumes of documentation, and the anti-Semitism of one's youth was exchanged for philo-Semitism, and one defined oneself unquestioningly and without risk as antifascist. But I, and many of my generation, did not take the time to think through fundamental questions, questions dictated with Old-Testament sternness, questions like: Can one do art after Auschwitz? Is it permissible to write poems after Auschwitz?

There was the dictum by Theodor Adorno: "To write a poem after Auschwitz is barbarous, and also undermines our understanding of why it has become impossible to write poems nowadays." Since 1951 a book by Adorno had been available — *Minima Moralia: Reflections from a Damaged Life,* where for the first time, to my knowledge, Auschwitz was seen as a great divide, an irreparable tear in the history of civilization. Yet this new categorical imperative was promptly misunderstood to be a prohibition. A prohibition like other stern prohibitions standing in the way of the thirst for change and the belief, apparently undamaged, in the future. An uncomfortable imperative, off-putting in its abstractness, and easy to circumvent.

Before people took the time to examine Adorno's remarks within the context of the reflections that preceded and followed them, and thus to realize that they were not a prohibition but a standard to be met, resistance to them had already consolidated. The abbreviated Adorno statement, that no poem should be written after Auschwitz, was refuted in a similarly abbreviated and unthinking form, as if enemies were exchanging blows. Adorno's prohibition was declared barbarous; it asked too much of human beings; it was inhumane; after all, life, no matter how damaged, had to go on.

My reaction, too, based on ignorance — on hearsay only — was to oppose it. Feeling myself in full possession of my powers, of my unique talents, I wanted to give them free rein, to prove them. Adorno's prohibition struck me as unnatural, as if someone had had the godthefatherly audacity to forbid birds to sing.

Was it defiance again or my old unwavering certainty that led me to dismiss Adorno so quickly? Didn't I know from personal experience what had horrified me and now haunted me? Why not put aside, if only for a short while, my sculpting, and impose a Lenten fast on my lyrical imagination, that greedy lodger within me?

Today I suspect that Adorno affected me more strongly than I could admit at the time. Something had been stirred up in me, and despite my resistance a control had been placed over me. The freedom of creativity, thought to be unlimited, a thing not won but handed to us, had come under surveillance.

Leafing through my writings, to see what that art student, apparently obsessed only with art, was up to, I find a poem written during those years; it was published in final form in 1960, in the poetry volume *Gleisdreieck,* but should really have appeared in my first book, *Die Vorzüge der Windhühner.* It is called "Askesis," and is a programmatic poem, expressing the feeling of grayness that to me is still basic:

> The cat speaks.
> And what does the cat say?
> Thou shalt draw with sharpened pencil
> brides of shade and shade of snow,
> thou shalt love the color gray
> and be beneath a cloudy sky.
>
> The cat speaks.
> And what does the cat say?
> Thou shalt be clad in the evening paper,
> clad in sackcloth like potatoes,
> and thou shalt turn this suit year out year in,
> and in a new suit never be.
>
> The cat speaks.
> And what does the cat say?
> Thou shouldst scratch the navy out;
> cherries, poppy, bloody nose

thou shalt scratch out, that flag as well,
and daub geraniums with ash.

Thou, the cat goes on to say,
shalt live on kidneys, spleen and liver,
lung that's out of breath and sour,
on urine of unsoaked kidneys
old spleen and tough liver
out of a gray pot: live on that.

And on the wall, where earlier without pause
the ruminant green picture chewed its green,
thou shalt write with thy sharp pencil
this: Askesis; write: Askesis.
That's what the cat says: write Askesis.[1]

I have quoted these five stanzas to you not to feed the
German literature professors' delight in interpretation, but
because the poem, I believe, gives an indirect answer to
Adorno's imperative by setting limits to its own undertak-
ing, in the form of a circumscribing reflex. Because even
though I, along with many others, had misunderstood Adorno's imperative as a prohibition, its signpost, marking the
divide, was still clearly visible.

All of us, the young poets of the fifties—let me name
Peter Rühmkorf, Hans Magnus Enzensberger, also Ingeborg
Bachmann—were aware, some clearly, some vaguely, that
we belonged to the Auschwitz generation—not as crimi-

---

1. *Selected Poems,* trans. Michael Hamburger and Christopher Middleton (Harcourt
Brace Jovanovich, 1977), p. 43.

nals, to be sure, but in the camp of the criminals. That in our biography, therefore, among the usual dates was written the date of the Wannsee Conference.[2] But we also knew this much: that Adorno's imperative could be refuted, if at all, only by writing.

But how? From whom should we learn? From Brecht? Benn? The early Expressionists? What tradition should we adopt, what criteria? The minute I picture myself as a young poetic talent next to the young Enzensberger and Rühmkorf, I realize that our headstart—and talent is nothing but a headstart—was playful, artistic, art-infatuated to the point of artificiality, and would probably have played itself out in a manner not worth mentioning if we had not had leaden shackles placed on us at the right moment. One of those shackles, which we wore even as we refused to wear it, was Theodor Adorno's imperative. I took my course from his signpost. And that course called for renouncing color; it called for gray in all gray's endless shadings.

It meant abandoning absolutes, the black and white of ideology, it meant showing belief the door and placing all one's bets on doubt, which turned everything, even the rainbow, to gray. But this imperative yielded wealth of another sort: the heartrending beauty of all the shades of gray was to be celebrated in damaged language. That meant hauling down one's flag and daubing the geraniums with ash. That meant drawing with sharpened pencil and scrawling on that wall, where "earlier without pause the ruminant

2. At the Wannsee Conference, held January 20, 1942, the National Socialists met to plan the "final solution" of the Jewish Question.

green picture chewed its green," Askesis as my watch-
word.

So away with the blues of introspection, the piling up
of metaphors, the infection with Rilkesque vagueness, and
polished literary chamber music. Askesis meant distrust of
sing-song sounds, of the lyrical timelessness of the nature
worshipers who in the fifties cultivated their garden patches
and supplied the schoolbooks with value-free constructs of
meaning, rhymed or unrhymed. Askesis also meant selecting
a point of view. From this insight dates my commitment (it
was during the argument between Sartre and Camus) to
Sisyphus, the happy boulder-pusher.

At the beginning of 1953 I changed locales and teachers.
Nothing to it: from Düsseldorf, the capital of the economic
miracle just then breaking out, to Berlin, by inter-zone train.
A heap of poems, my chisels, a clean shirt, a few books and
records — that was my luggage.

Berlin, smashed but already occupied by ideologies again,
seemed to revive from crisis to crisis; it sprawled flat between mountains of ruins. Emptied squares, in which the
wind swirled twisters of debris. Brick dust between one's
teeth. Arguments about everything. Representational versus
nonrepresentational art: Hofer on one side, Grohmann on
the other. Over here and over there: here Benn, there Brecht.
Cold war by loudspeaker. And yet the Berlin of those years,
for all the shouting, was a place as silent as the dead. Time
had refused to be speeded up. The "damaged life" was still
a reality not obscured by discount offers. In Berlin there
was no patience for flirting with the unspeakable. My last

imitative finger exercises were corrected by a stern rubber eraser. Here, things wanted to be called by name.

In quick succession, away from the modeling stand and drawing board, I turned out my first independent poems, verses that performed their acrobatics freestyle and without a net, so to speak. I also wrote dialogues, brief one-act plays. One of them later became the last act of a four-act play titled *Mister, Mister*. This is how it begins:

The outskirts of the city. An abandoned building site. Piles of gravel, scaffolding. Bollin is standing on a mortar pail. He looks expectantly in the direction of the city. Sprat and Slick approach slowly.

SPRAT: Mister?
SLICK: Mister, aintcha got a thing?
SPRAT: Yeah, mister, give it here.
SLICK: Aintcha? Just one?
SPRAT: Hey, mister.
SLICK: You deaf?
BOLLIN: No!
SLICK: Only one, mister.
BOLLIN: I ain't got nothing.
SPRAT: Take a look. Maybe you got sumpin.
BOLLIN: Such as what?
SPRAT: Just a thing.
BOLLIN: What kind of a thing?
SPRAT: Everybody's got sumpin.

SLICK: Why wouldn't you?

BOLLIN: Take my word for it, kids, I haven't. . . .[3]

And three years later, in the spring of 1956—I'm still studying sculpture with Karl Hartung—my first book of poems and drawings appears, with quatrains such as this one:

GASAG

In our suburb
A toad is sitting on the gas meter.
It breathes in and out
So we can cook.

Today I ask myself: Is that the kind of poem, the kind of dialogue it was permissible to write after Auschwitz? Did the imperative for askesis have to result in such an anorexic form? I was now twenty-eight years old, but for the time being I couldn't do more than this, or anything different.

And I read my poems and one-act plays at the meetings of Group 47, which in the person of Hans Werner Richter regularly invited me, the beginner, from the fall of 1955 on. Many of the manuscripts read there were more outspoken than mine. Some of them attacked National Socialism, as if to make up for lost time, unambiguously, with the help of positive heroes. The lack of ambiguity made me nervous. Such belated antifascism had the sound of a required exercise, conformist in a time of abject conformism, hence dis-

3. *Four Plays,* trans. Ralph Manheim and A. Leslie Willson (Harcourt Brace & World, 1967), pp. 146–147.

honest, and positively obscene when compared with the real resistance to National Socialism, a resistance which, though doomed to failure and pathetically weak, had left real traces.

These first experiences with literature and what goes on around it caused me to regress. I was seventeen again. The end of the war. The unconditional surrender. Imprisoned in foxholes. Photographs showing piles of eyeglasses, shoes, bones. My stubborn refusal to believe it. And turning the counter back even farther: fifteen, fourteen, thirteen years old. Campfires, flag drills, shooting practice with small-caliber weapons. The dull routine of school interrupted by vacations, while the news came in special bulletins. Certainly: schoolboy defiance, boredom during Hitler Youth exercises. Stupid jokes about the party bigwigs, who dodged service at the front and were mockingly called "golden pheasants." But resistance? Not a trace, not even the stirring of resistance, not even in the most fleeting thoughts. Instead, admiration for military heroes and a persistent mindless credulity that nothing could put a dent in. An embarrassment even today.

How could I think to capture resistance on paper ten years later, ascribing antifascism to myself, when "writing after Auschwitz" had shame, shame on every white page as its prerequisite? Rather, what emerged from the fifties was opposition to the scale of new false notes, to the façade-art flourishing all around, to smug gatherings of complacent Philistines—if some of them had known nothing, guessed nothing, and now presented themselves as children seduced by demonic forces, the others had always been against it, if not out loud then at least in secret.

A decade of lies that even today have market value, but a decade, too, of momentous decisions. Rearmament and the German Treaty were the key words here. Two German states were coming into being, tit for tat, each zealously trying to be the model pupil in its respective political bloc, each delighted at being fortunate to count itself among the victors. Divided, yes, but united in the perception of having survived one more time.

Yet one element did not fit into this picture of hostile twosomeness. On June 16 and 17, 1953, the workers were on the march in East Berlin and Leipzig, in Halle, Bitterfeld, and Magdeburg. The streets belonged to them until the Soviet tanks came. A strike on Stalinallee (Stalin had died the previous March) grew into an uprising, which took a sad course, leaderless and carried out only by workers. No intellectuals, no students, no professionals, and no church leaders joined in, only a few members of the People's Police, who were later court-martialed and shot. And yet this German workers' uprising, to which Albert Camus paid his respects from Paris, was covered up—made into a counterrevolution over there, and over here, by the words of the liar Adenauer, into a people's uprising and an excuse to create a holiday.

I watched it. From Potsdamer Platz I saw tanks and human beings face off. A decade later, an eyewitness of that brief confrontation, I wrote a German tragedy in complex form—*The Plebeians Rehearse the Uprising*—complex because integrated into the play were Shakespeare's *Coriolanus* and Brecht's *Coriolanus* adaptation, as well as his position on the seventeenth of June. But complex, too, because the reality of the street — a leaderless uprising — contradicts the reality of a theater rehearsal, which is dedicated to raising revolutionary consciousness, particularly that of the working class. And complex, furthermore, because the head of the theater on whose stage the tragedy takes place is never unambiguous — or is unable to be. When, near the end of the play, he finally decides to write a letter of protest to the first secretary of the central committee — at the time, Walter Ulbricht — he is opposed by an actress, Volumnia, and his dramatic adviser Erwin:

> VOLUMNIA *takes the paper away from him:* Why read this pussyfooting document aloud? Three succinct paragraphs. The first two are critical; you say the measures taken by the government, in other words the Party, were premature. In the third, something makes you proclaim your solidarity with the same people you attacked in the first two. Why not come out for Kozanka in the first place? Because they'll cross out the critical paragraphs and trumpet the solidarity until you die of shame.

> BOSS: Here, underneath the original, I have a copy. Blessed be carbon paper.

> ERWIN: Those things are locked up in the archives; they get published with your posthumous papers when it's too late.

VOLUMNIA: And legends will grow up. Deep down he was against. Or deep down he was for. That's the way he spoke, but his heart—hm, what about his heart? Everybody will have his own interpretation: cynical opportunist, home-grown idealist; all he really cared about was theater; he wrote and thought for the people. What people? Speak out. Give them a piece of your mind or knuckle under. And dovetail your sentences, don't leave an opening for their scissors.

BOSS: No one will censor me.

VOLUMNIA: Don't be childish. You know perfectly well you're going to be cut.

ERWIN: And even uncut it's feeble. Did you really write this? It's feeble, it's embarrassing.

BOSS: Like the subject matter. Do you want me to write: I congratulate the meritorious murderers of the people. Or I congratulate the ignorant survivors of a feeble uprising. And what congratulations will reach the dead? And I, capable of nothing but small, embarrassed words, stood on the sidelines. Masons, railroad workers, welders and cable winders remained alone. Housewives didn't hang back. Even some of the Vopos threw off their belts. They'll be court-martialed. In our camp they'll add new wings to the prisons. And in the Western camp, too, lies will become official truths. The face of hypocrisy will rehearse in a display of mourning. My farseeing eye sees national rags falling to half-mast. I can hear whole platoons of orators sucking the word "freedom" empty. I can see the years hobbling by. And after the fatal calendar leaf has been plucked ten or twelve times, they'll take to celebrating the seventeenth with beer orgies as they celebrated the Battle of Sedan in my childhood. In the West I see a well-fed nation picnicking in the green. What's left? Bottles drained in celebration, sandwich papers, beer corpses and real corpses: for on holidays the traffic takes its meed of corpses. But here, after ten or twelve years, the prisons will vomit up the wreckage of this uprising. Accusation will run rampant, address and mail a thousand packages of guilt. We've got our package ready. *Hands the original and copy to Litthenner and Podulla.* Kindly play the messengers. The original to the Central Committee; the copy to friends in the West for safekeeping.

PODULLA: Boss, they'll say we're sitting on the fence.

BOSS: Answer, what better seat have you to offer?[4]

This play stuck in the craw of the critics in both East and West when it premiered in January 1966 at the Schillerthea-

---

4. *The Plebeians Rehearse the Uprising,* trans. Ralph Manheim (Harcourt, Brace and World, 1966), p. 107ff.

ter in Berlin. Over there it was dismissed as "counterrevolutionary," over here as an "anti-Brecht play." It soon disappeared from the theaters. But encouraged by the present revolutionary developments, the author now places a bet on the longevity of his *Plebeians*.

But I am getting ahead of myself. The twenty-five-year-old witness of June 17, 1953 had not yet reached the point where he could react by writing directly. Things of the past, losses, his origins, shame still clung to him. It was not until three years later, when I moved from Berlin to Paris, that the distance from Germany enabled me to find the language and the breath to write down in fifteen hundred pages what was necessary for me to write, in spite of and after Auschwitz. Driven by the recklessness that is specific to the profession, and by a persistent writing frenzy, I completed—without interruption, though in several versions, in Paris and then Berlin after my return in 1960—*The Tin Drum, Cat and Mouse,* and *Dog Years.*

No writer, I would assert, will undertake a major epic without being pushed, provoked, and lured by others into that great avalanche zone. In Cologne, when I was passing through, it was Paul Schallück who gave me the push to write prose. The provocation came from the current pervasive, even official, demonization of the Nazi period—I wanted to illuminate the crime, bring it into the open—and I was lured into continuing, after relapses, by a difficult, almost inaccessible friend, Paul Celan, who understood sooner than I did that the first book, with its 730 galloping pages, did not tell the whole story, but rather that this profane epic onion had to be unpeeled layer by layer, and that I must not take a break from the peeling. He gave me the courage to include fictional characters like Fajngold, Sigismund Markus, and Eddi Amsel—not noble but ordinary and eccentric Jews—in the petty-bourgeois world of my novels.

Why Paul Celan, for whom words became increasingly spare toward the end of the fifties, and whose language and existence were narrowing into a fuguelike stretto? His help was never given directly, but was slipped into subordinate clauses during a walk in the park. His encouragement and intervention affected *Dog Years* more than *The Tin Drum*—for example, at the beginning of the fairy tale near the end of the second part, when a mountain of bones is piled up next to the Kaiserhafen antiaircraft battery, which mountain is fed by the Stutthof concentration camp near Danzig:

There once was a girl, her name was Tulla,

and she had the pure forehead of a child. But nothing is pure. Not even the snow is pure. No virgin is pure. Even a pig isn't pure. The Devil never entirely pure. No note rises pure. Every violin knows that. Every star chimes that. Every knife peels it: even a potato isn't pure: it has eyes, they have to be scooped out.

But what about salt? Salt is pure! Nothing, not even salt, is pure. It's only on boxes that it says: Salt is pure. After all, it keeps. What keeps with it? But it's washed. Nothing can be washed clean. But the elements: pure? They are sterile but not pure. The idea? Isn't it always pure? Even in the beginning not pure. Jesus Christ not pure. Marx Engels not pure. Ashes not pure. And the host not pure. No idea stays pure. Even the flowering of art isn't pure. And the sun has spots. All geniuses menstruate. On sorrow floats laughter. In the heart of roaring lurks silence. In angles lean compasses. But the circle, the circle is pure!

No closing of the circle is pure. For if the circle is pure, then the snow is pure, the virgin is, pigs are, Jesus Christ, Marx and Engels, white ashes, all sorrows, laughter, to the left roaring, to the right silence, ideas immaculate, wafers no longer bleeders and geniuses without efflux, all angles pure angles, piously compasses would describe circles: pure and human, dirty, salty, diabolical, Christian and Marxist, laughing and roaring, ruminant, silent, holy, round pure angular. And the bones, white mounds that were recently heaped up, would grow immaculately without crows: pyramids of glory. But the crows, which are not pure, were creaking unoiled, even yesterday: nothing is pure, no circle, no bone. And piles of bones, heaped up for the sake of purity, will melt cook boil in order that soap, pure and cheap; but even soap cannot wash pure.[5]

With the novel *Dog Years*—which, I don't know why, must parade its unwieldiness in the shadow of *The Tin Drum* but

5. *Dog Years,* trans. Ralph Manheim (Harcourt Brace & World, 1965), pp. 295–296.

has remained dear to its author, and not only for that reason—my prose projects were completed for the time being.
Not that I was exhausted; but I believed that I had written
myself free of something, something that was now behind
me, not settled, to be sure, yet dealt with.

Last summer Hessian State Radio gave me the opportunity to read the entire *Tin Drum* aloud, over the course of
twelve evenings, to an audience in Göttingen. A great strain
to take upon myself, but I had the pleasure, as I reread the
book, of looking over the shoulder of the young writer and
seeing how he turned an idea from a play that never got
written into the epilogue of the Polish Post Office, the house-
of-cards chapter. And seeing where the term "fizz powder"
first insisted on being remembered. And recalling which vis-
itors to Paris had heard the first draft of which *Tin Drum*
chapters—Walter Höllerer again and again; and how little
he was disturbed by the periodic reports of the death of the
novel.

Thirty years later, it is easy for me to say that later
everything became more difficult. Bored with itself, fame
stood in the way. Friendships fell apart. Reviewers panting
with specific expectations insisted that my sole subject should
be Danzig, only Danzig, with its flat and hilly environs.
Whenever I turned to the present, whether with *The Plebeians*
or with prose again—*Local Anaesthetic* and *From the Diary of a
Snail*—or if I got involved in a German election campaign,
down to all the provincial details, and took an active role in
politics as a citizen, their judgment was sure to fall: He
should stick to Danzig and his Kashubians. Politics has brought

nothing but harm to writers. Goethe knew that. And other such schoolmasterly admonitions.

But writing after Auschwitz could not and cannot be dealt with so solicitously. The past casts its hard shadows over present and future terrain — I later coined the term "pastpresentfuture" and tried out that concept in *Diary of a Snail.* Inspired by Heine's fragment, "The Rabbi of Bacharach," I wanted to describe the history of the Danzig synagogue congregation up to its liquidation — once again digging up the past — but I also had a mission in the present: the 1969 election campaign was clouded by an agreement that a former National Socialist would be acceptable as chancellor for the Great Coalition. And there was a third narrative level: laying the foundation for an essay on Albrecht Dürer's copper engraving "Melencolia I," an essay to be titled "On Stasis in Progress." The form of this diary, set therefore in the present, past, and future, was determined by my children's questions:

> "Where are you off to again tomorrow?"
> "Castrop-Rauxel."
> "What are you going to do there?"
> "Talktalktalk."
> "Still the same old S.P.D.?"
> "It's just beginning."
> "And what'll you bring us this time?"
> "Myself, among other things . . ."
> . . . and the question: Why those streaks on the wallpaper? (Everything that backs up with the tripe and coats the palate with tallow.)

Because, sometimes, children, at table, or when the TV throws out a word (about Biafra), I hear Franz or Raoul asking about the Jews:

"What about them? What's the story?"

You notice that I falter whenever I abbreviate. I can't find the needle's eye, and I start babbling.

Because this, but first that, and meanwhile the other, but only after . . .

I try to thin out forests of facts before they have time for new growth. To cut holes in the ice and keep them open. Not to sew up the gap. Not to tolerate jumps entailing a frivolous departure from history, which is a landscape inhabited by snails . . .

"Exactly how many were they?"
"How did they count them?"

It was a mistake to give you the total, the multidigitate number. It was a mistake to give the mechanism a numerical value, because perfect killing arouses hunger for technical details and suggests questions about breakdowns.

"Did it always work?"
"What kind of gas was it?"

Illustrated books and documents. Anti-Fascist memorials built in the Stalinist style. Badges of repentance and brotherhood weeks. Well-lubricated words of repentance. Detergents and all-purpose poetry: "When night fell over Germany . . ."

Now I'll tell you (and go on telling you as long as the election campaign goes on and Kiesinger is Chancellor) how it happened where I come from— slowly, deliberately, and in broad daylight. Preparations for the universal crime were made in many places at the same time though at unequal speeds; in Danzig, which before the war did not belong to the German Reich, the process was slowed down, which made it easier to record later on. . . .[6]

In this book, which appeared in Germany in 1972, the definition of my profession is asked for, and the reply is given: "A writer, children, is someone who writes against passing time." Which means that the author sees himself not as independent of time or encapsulated in timelessness, but as a contemporary. More, that he exposes himself to vicissitudes, gets involved, and takes sides. The dangers of such involvement and side-taking are known: the writer's objectivity may be lost; his language is tempted to live from hand to mouth; the narrowness of present circumstances may prove confining to his imaginative powers, which are accustomed to run free; he risks getting out of breath.

Possibly because I was aware of the dangers of my declared contemporariness, I was already secretly writing an-

6. *From the Diary of a Snail,* trans. Ralph Manheim (Harcourt Brace Jovanovich, 1973), pp. 11–12.

other book——behind my own back, as it were——while doing the first draft of the snail diary, while on the road in the election campaign, making speeches and listening to myself making speeches. It was a book that allowed me to unreel history backward and send the language to fairy-tale school. As if I had wanted to recover from the snail and from the programmatic slowness of my snail-party, I began——no sooner than the diary had appeared, and I had savored another election campaign through to the first computer projection of the outcome——with the preliminary work on another epic tome, *The Flounder.*

What does this book have to do with my topic, "Writing after Auschwitz"? It deals with food, from barley gruel to cutlet in aspic. It deals with surpluses and shortages, with gluttony and gnawing hunger. It deals with nine or more cooks and the other truth of that fairy tale "The Fisherman and His Wife": how man in his desire for mastery always wants more, wants to be faster, climb higher, how he sets himself final goals, works for the final solution, is "at the end." "At the end" is the title of one of the poems that impede the flow of prose in *The Flounder,* either to summarize or switch onto another track:

Men, who with that well-known expression
Think things to the end
and have always thought them to the end;
men for whom not possibly possible goals
but the ultimate goal——a society free
from care——

has pitched its tent beyond mass graves;
men who from the sum of dated defeats
draw only one conclusion: smoke-veiled
       ultimate victory
over radically scorched earth;
men who at one of those conferences
held daily since the worst proved to
       be technically
feasible
resolve with masculine realism on
the final solution;
men with perspective,
men goaded by importance,
great exalted men,
whom no one and no warm slippers
can hold,
men with precipitous ideas followed
       by flat deeds —
have we finally — we wonder — seen
       the last of them?[7]

Here, if not sooner, I notice that the topic of my talk keeps forcing me to give an account of myself, even when a story like *Meeting in Telgte* speaks for itself. The backdating of Group 47, that literary non-club to which I owe much, could be undertaken effortlessly, was even child's play.

    The situation was different with a book that was supposed to ring in Orwell's decade, the eighties: *Headbirths* —

7. *The Flounder*, trans. Ralph Manheim (Harcourt Brace Jovanovich, 1978), pp. 95–96.

or the Germans are Dying Out. As with the *Flounder,* in the chapter "Vasco Returns" it is no longer Europe, or the double Germany, and certainly not Danzig-Gdańsk that is the measure of all things. Rather, it is the ever more rapidly growing and increasingly impoverished population of Asia and the so-called north-south differential that pressure the narrative to make utopian leaps. Because even from the perspective of China, Indonesia, and India, our old continent shrinks to the size of a toy, the "German Question" finally reveals its third-rate status, and the literature that was wrested from the aftermath of Auschwitz again becomes questionable.

Where can literature still find an outlet if the future has already been dated, the terrible statistical bottom line calculated? What is left to narrate if the human race's capacity for destroying itself and all other life in a multitude of ways is proven daily and practiced in computer simulations? Nothing. Yet the atomic self-annihilation, which might come at any hour, relates to Auschwitz and expands the "final solution" to global dimensions.

A writer who reaches this conclusion—and from the beginning of the eighties the renewed arms race points to such a conclusion—must either make silence his imperative, or else—and after three years of abstinence I began to work on a novel again—try to give a name to this human possibility, self-annihilation.

The Rat, a book in which "I dreamed I had to say good-bye," was an attempt, then, to continue the crippled project of the Enlightenment. But the Zeitgeist, and with it the highly paid jabbering of a culture business mightily pleased

with itself, refused to be needled. Art fairs pushing one another from the market, overdirected theatrical perfor-
mances, and the gigantomania of provincial tycoons who have
recently discovered art are features of the eighties. The en-
tertaining bustle of mediocrity and its talkshow hosts, who
can say absolutely anything but are not allowed to pause,
lest they fall into shocked silence — all this dynamic mind-
lessness did not begin to stumble until, beyond the pale of
this doubly fortified prosperity, the peoples of Eastern and
Central Europe rose up, one after the other, and gave new
meaning to old-fashioned words like solidarity and freedom.

Since then something has happened. The West stands
naked. The cry over there, "We are the people," found no
echo over here. "We are already free," people here said.
"We already have everything, the only thing missing is unity."
And thus a thing that yesterday raised hopes and brought
Europe into focus becomes twisted into German aspirations.
Once again the call is heard for "all of Germany."

Since I have given my lecture the ponderous title "Writing
after Auschwitz," and have drawn up a literary balance sheet,
I want — in closing — to confront the break in civilization
epitomized by Auschwitz with the German longing for reunification. Auschwitz speaks against every trend born of
manipulation of public opinion, against the purchasing power
of the West German economy — for the hard currency of
Deutschmarks even unification can be acquired — and yes,
even against the right to self-determination granted without
hesitation to other peoples. Auschwitz speaks against all this,
because one of the preconditions for the terrible thing that
happened was a strong, unified Germany.

Writing after Auschwitz

By themselves not Prussia, not Bavaria, not even Austria could have developed the methodology and the will for organized genocide, and implemented it; it had to be all of Germany. We have every reason to fear ourselves as a unit. Nothing, no sense of nationhood, however idyllically colored, and no assurance of late-born benevolence can modify or dispel the experience that we the criminals, with our victims, had as a unified Germany. We cannot get around Auschwitz. And no matter how greatly we want to, we should not attempt to get around it, because Auschwitz belongs to us, is a permanent stigma of our history—and a positive gain! It has made possible this insight: Finally we know ourselves.

Thinking about Germany is also part of my literary work. Since the mid-sixties and into the present continuing turmoil, there have been occasions for speeches and essays. Often my necessarily cutting remarks have struck my contemporaries as excessive interference, as extraliterary meddling. That is not my concern. Rather, I am left with a sense of inadequacy after completing this thirty-five-year balance sheet. Something remains to be said that has not yet been put into words. An old story wants to be told altogether differently. Perhaps I will succeed in this task. My speech has to find its end, but there is no end to writing after Auschwitz, no such promise can be made—unless the human race gives up on itself completely.